A DAY IN THE LIFE

of a

TUSCANY
WINEMAKER

CONTINUING THE
CRAFT AND PASSION
OF OLD-WORLD
ITALIAN WINES

AL LAUTENSLAGER

Front Cover Design and Interior Layout
by Cathi Stevenson and Gwen Gades

© Cover Image Credits:
Man: @oliverhlavatyphotographie / depositphotos.com
Grapes and vineyard path: @mythja / depositphotos.com
Mountains by Bob Stevenson
Small grape leaf: Dover 922 Decorative
Vector Ornaments

Print: 978-1-7350723-1-9
eBook: 978-1-7350723-2-6

A DAY IN THE LIFE
of a
TUSCANY
WINEMAKER

CONTINUING THE
CRAFT AND PASSION
OF OLD-WORLD
ITALIAN WINES

AL LAUTENSLAGER

CONTENTS

PREFACE

LIFE IS FULL of experiences and pleasures. These can take many forms, including physical activity, leisure activities, and consumption. Pursuing one or more of these is what life is all about.

The category of food and drink is one of those pleasures. The more you are interested in it, the more you will want to learn. Your learning will fulfill you even more and in turn, cause you to want more. That's what this book is about.

Most people love a behind-the-scenes story. You are about to learn what happens behind the scenes of winemaking, specifically for winemakers in Tuscany. You will learn what the life of a Tuscan winemaker is like. You will grow in appreciation for those who make wine for you. You will obtain more than a conversational knowledge to talk about and to be able to better share your wine experiences. You will learn that wine is more than a standard drink order or beverage that goes with dinner.

At their core, a winemaker is a person who takes grapes and turns them into wine. However, due to the nearly limitless number of options a winemaker has to choose from, a winemaking career can differ widely from person to person.

In this book, you will hear from ten different winemakers about their varied day-to-day activity and life. Winemakers are in charge of the decisions of when to pick the grapes, what style of wine will be made, the aging of wine, and any blending decisions on the way to the perfect final wine. They monitor the maturity of grapes to ensure their quality and to determine the correct time for harvest.

This book is the only comprehensive guide to the lives of Tuscan winemakers. It surveys lifestyles, career path choices, family influences, tradition, and more, perfect for any and all Italian wine enthusiasts.

Fasten your seat belts and get ready to immerse yourself in their lives.

A Day in the Life of a Tuscany Winemaker – Continuing the Craft and Passion of Old World Italian Wines, is the perfect invitation to the Italian/Tuscan wine and winemaking experience.

INTRODUCTION

Tuscany is a state of grace. The countryside is so lovingly designed that the eye sweeps the mountains and valleys without stumbling over a single stone. The lilt of the rolling green hills, the upsurging cypresses, the terraces sculptured by generations that have handled the rocks with skillful tenderness, the fields geometrically juxtaposed as though drawn by a draughtsman for beauty as well as productivity; the battlements of castles on the hills, their tall towers standing grey-blue and golden tan among the forest of trees, the air of such clarity that every sod of earth stands out in such dazzling detail. The fields ripening with barley and oats, beans, and beets. The grape-heavy vines espaliered between the horizontal branches of silver-green olive trees, composing orchards of webbed design, rich in intimation of wine, olive oil and lacy-leaf poetry. Tuscany untied the knots in a man's intestines, wiped out the ills of the world. Italy is the garden of Europe, Tuscany is the garden of Italy, Florence is the flower of Tuscany."
- Irving Stone - *The Agony and the Ecstasy*

MENTION ITALY TO anyone and a multitude of images, thoughts, ideas, and visuals come to mind, many that tantalize the senses. Some are geographical in nature like the boot shape of the country. Others are experiential and are food and wine related. If you were to hear of some of the Italian feasts and celebrations, it's almost guaranteed that your mouth would start watering, kitchens would steam up, smells would be imagined and more, all in response to the power of Italian food and drink.

Some thoughts conjured would be of Renaissance history and art, Greco-Roman influences—geographical regions and countries that culturally are and were influenced by the languages, the arts, early forms of government and religion of the ancient Greeks and Romans.

Those of a historical mindset will quickly think of the Roman Empire, Da Vinci, Michelangelo, The Coliseum, The Vatican, Catholicism, and the popes when asked about top-of-mind thoughts related to Italy. Of course, your list could go on from here.

At the forefront of these lists and descriptions, in most cases, are the culinary delights, the flavors and the drink of the grapes. Pizza, lasagna, meatballs, and the many varietals of Italian red wine (and even whites) make up many Italian connotations, hopes, wishes, dreams, memories, and experiences.

People have filled entire journals with Italian food choices, their history, recipes, and predominance in the old and new world. Journals could also be filled with the many Italian wine stories, varieties, and products.

For the perfect fusion of food, wine, and culture, there is simply nowhere like Italy. It's no surprise that Italian winemaking has grown tremendously in popularity.

Setting aside culinary delights and influences, Italian wines come quickly into focus and many times to the forefront of this association. Many people can rattle off names of Italian wines—Prosecco, Chianti, Montalcino, Montepulciano, Lambrusco, Pinot Grigio, and more. None come more into focus in Italian wine surveys and inventory than those wines from the famous geographical area of Tuscany.

While this is not a book about Tuscany and Italian wine history, it will touch upon some history of the many inner territories of this central Italian region and some outlying territories with Florence, the most populated city in Tuscany, as its capital.

Geographically, cities most referenced when asked about Italy are Rome, Florence, and Venice. Of course, there are many more, but ask anyone where they visit most when traveling to this country and one of these three cities will be the reply.

Our focus here is on the Tuscany region,

which includes Florence.

No city or region in modern Europe has a grander history than Florence and Tuscany. From its extended Roman history, its reputation for prospering as a center of trade, commerce, and finance and being the birthplace of the Italian Renaissance, Florence and Tuscany towers above the rest as the leading Italian region.

Whether you've just begun to explore wine or are an expert who appreciates and understands Tuscan wine, this will serve as a behind-the-scenes look at the production of the quality wines that you know about or want to know about.

At the end of the day, Italy is all about art, culture, food, family, and traditions. Understanding Tuscan winemaking will surely broaden your horizons in this area.

You don't have to be a student of history to appreciate that there is something special about knowing the facts, the stories, the people, and nuances behind what you eat, drink, wear, and use in your everyday life, and that includes wine. Thinking about how winemaking began can spark your imagination and help put things in the proper perspective and regard. Making the connection from the world's very first winemaking experience to your latest taste of an Italian vintage, gives you a more real experience and a deeper appreciation, meaning, and sense of enjoyment and delight with Italian wines.

This book is not a primer on Chianti wine or even Tuscany wines, per se. This is a book about people and their lives. Much knowledge will come from the personal stories, lessons, experiences, and craft discussions offered. It is about the life surrounding the wines: the culture and experiences of Tuscan inhabitants, families, workers, and especially Tuscan winemakers.

With all of this in mind, join us here as we take a walk through Italian/Tuscan winemaking, the people involved, their lives surrounding winemaking and more, historically to present day.

WINE PASSION

ACCORDING TO THE Merriam-Webster Dictionary, passion is defined as a strong and barely controllable emotion. Wikipedia defines passion as a feeling of intense enthusiasm towards or compelling desire for someone or something. Passion can range from eager interest in or admiration for an idea, proposal, or cause, to enthusiastic enjoyment of an interest or activity. Does the thought of wine come to mind yet? What about Italian food and culture?

This definition certainly applies to wine drinkers and winemakers around the world and in Tuscany. They have an intense enthusiasm, a compelling desire, an eager interest, an admiration for an idea and enthusiastic enjoyment related to wine drinking and winemaking. Extending the Merriam-Webster definition to wine, passion is defined as a strong and barely controllable emotion when it comes to wine. It has been further observed that passion is present when it comes to making wine, drinking wine, sharing wine, talking about wine, and learning about wine. That is wine passion.

Winemakers are wine lovers and they will take every opportunity to brag, promote, and advocate their passion by sharing, serving, tasting, and pairing wine with their favorite foods. They will talk endlessly about their favorite grapes, vintages, methods, and regions all while engaging with consumers. Nothing fuels this more than real life experiences with all of the above.

This is not an overstatement when it comes to passion for wine.

Letwine.com states that, "Wine is not just a drink or a hobby for many, but a passion that engages all the senses. It is complete and tells the story of a territory and its history." This alone captures wine passion for sure, whether in Tuscany or any other part of the wine world.

Jean-Charles Boisset, author of *Passion for Wine*, claims that his medium is passion and he is considered one of the modern wine industry's great impresarios. He encourages us to get back to the real reason we drink wine: That is for the sheer pleasure of it.

Today you can walk into a wine bar or a wine

tasting and see so many so-called wine aficionados uptight and unable to relax and truly enjoy
what wine is all about because they are fearful
they will not follow etiquette rules or will say
something inappropriate amongst other wine
drinkers. They worry about the wine rating
number. They need to take Jean-Charles Boisset's advice to relax and enjoy wine's pleasures,
whatever they are to the appreciating wine
drinker: a true appreciation of pleasure and
passion; a true savoring of what is in the glass; a
true appreciation of what it took to turn a grape
into what's in the glass.

What keeps this conversation and pursuit
going? The one-word simple answer is Passion.
Passion for a drink that has persisted and flourished for thousands of years. The passion that
surrounds growing vines that bear fruit that
goes through a process to yield what goes into
the wine bottles around the world. Others have
described the enthusiasm as passion for the
comfort, joy, and ecstasy of the greatest glass of
something on earth.

This passion transfers directly to winemaking for the winemaker. It becomes their life.
They physically toil and mentally grind. They
win some seasons and lose some, and almost
every winemaker wouldn't trade all of this for
the world. They do the job over and over. They
are passionate about their craft.

Perhaps the word passion is slightly over-used but never when it comes to the sacrifices that go into a bottle of wine, the joy felt when you see the fruits of labor condensed into one perfect bottle. Even those who are not in the profession of winemaking but make wine for personal use, even they appreciate the story that is behind the label of the bottle resting on its shelf.

At the end of the day, the passion for wine-making provides a personal return—when all of the winemaker's hard work brings joy to the many that truly enjoy the fruits of their labor. That's the passion a winemaker lives for and the passion that they remember day in and day out.

Letitwine.com says it best: "Drinking wine means being together and enjoying memorable moments." It is this idea which expresses the passion behind wine—the togetherness it creates within friendship and love. Whether they be old relationships or newly formed over a good bottle of wine, they are always found those evenings when you're looking for that smile or that spark which makes everything more memorable. Letitwine.com hits the nail on the head when it states, "Through a bottle, you can communicate everything."

Edmondo De Amicis, an Italian novelist, journalist, poet, and short-story writer describes what it means to be a wine lover: "Wine adds a smile to friendships and a spark to love. It is the second blood of the human race."

Wine is a journey and can be a collection of stories. Wine brings together different worlds which cross paths at the point of passion, at the point of wine passion. Wine is a moment of happiness.

Many have said in one form or another that when you live your passions, you live a life worth remembering.

WHY DO PEOPLE LIKE ITALIAN WINE?

THERE ARE MANY reasons to love Italy: its wines, food, language, architecture, art, people, history, landscapes, travel destinations... the list is endless. Those reasons have been mentioned and most will be mentioned and discussed again, if not continuously.

Let's focus here on wine and the appeal of wine, specifically Italian wine.

One has to wonder why Italian wines are so appealing; why are they on the aforementioned list of reasons to love Italy?

Italy is noted for its wine not because everyone is making wine in their own Italian villa or estate but because there are more native Italian grapes in Italy than any other European country. Italy's native grapes include and account for roughly 25% of the world's wine grapes, more than the grapes of France, Greece, and Spain combined.

Tourists visit this country annually to see what it is with Italian wine that makes it taste so good. The natives as well as the tourists will tell you that once you taste Italian wine, there is no going back. You will probably forever drink Italian wine. That, for sure, is the known effect it has on people.

Italy is essentially located in the perfect place on the planet for the abundant offering and thriving of wine grapes. Every grape and winery reviewed in this book has their own distinctive and unique appeal, character, taste, and quality. With some estimates of 2,000 native grape varietals in Italy, there is certainly an Italian grape and wine to satisfy any person's palate and preferences.

Let's dig deeper as to why people like Italian wine.

Italian food is by far the most chosen and favored cuisine in the world. People love Italian food. Don't believe that? Just ask the next person you talk to or the person sitting by you what they think about Italian food. The innovativeness and creativity of Italian people, both trained chefs and family cooks, create contributions and combinations that result in the distinction of Italian food as the world's favorite food.

The reasons why Italian meals are considered the best food in the world are virtually the same or at least very similar to the reasons why Italy has the best wines in the world. A major contributing factor to both is the biodiversity of Italy's soils, the wide variability of climatic conditions from the cold and snowy Alps in Northern Italy to the volcanic silt, fossil-like sands of Sicily in the South.

As part of Italian lore and a way of life, it is almost mandated that "thy shall drink wine with food." Mention a food and an Italian will tell you what wine goes with it. Mention a wine and an Italian will tell you what food pairs best with it. While many Italian wines can be consumed on their own and without food, it is a known and experienced fact that Italian wines can turn a good meal into a great meal and a great meal into a memorable experience. Italian wines and these experiences touch just about all of the senses which is another reason why Italian wine is the best and why people choose to drink it, Italians and non-Italians.

Another view as to why people enjoy drinking Italian wine is that they realize what is really being tasted, the satisfaction and delight when a wine meets and exceeds expectations, coupled with other outside influences that affect the likeability and tasting as much, sometimes, as the wine itself.

New Yorker Magazine psychology and science blogger Maria Konnikova published a post devoted to "what we really taste when we taste wine."

Konnikova states that, "No event or object is ever experienced in perfect, objective isolation. It is instead subject to our past experiences, our current mood, our expectations, and any number of incidental details—an annoying neighbor, a waiter who keeps banging your chair, a beautiful painting in your line of sight. With something like wine, all sorts of societal and personal complications come into play, as well. We worry, for example, about whether our taste is 'good.'"

"Expectations," writes Konnikova, "can influence our experience in two interrelated ways. There is the conscious influence, or those things we are knowingly aware of: I've had this wine before and liked or hated it; I've been to this vineyard; I love this grape; the color reminds me of a wine I had earlier that was delicious. As our experience grows, so do our expectations. Every time we have a wine, we taste everything we know about it and other related wines."

This does beg the question as to what role the wine itself plays in the taste and the reasons people like Italian wines. Let's dig deeper with the specific qualities of a Tuscan Chianti.

When drinking Chianti, most find a basic, earthy, rustic wine that's high in tannins.

Tannins, in Chianti's case are described as a true dryness, sometimes bitter and/or acidic. Although mostly in Italian red wine, it is considered to be the opposite flavoring as the sweet tastes of many white wines. Tannins, as part of Chiantis are not necessarily bad qualities or exceptional qualities. They are part of its character and part of what you expect, realize, experience, and remember.

This is furthered by a scent and taste that will remind you of forest fruits (berries), cherries, and strawberries. Sometimes a taste of smokiness and woodsy flavors surface. With elevated acidity, Chianti becomes the perfect wine to pair with just about any food you choose to pair it with, especially tomato sauces, pizzas, pastas and other traditional Italian dishes. Pairings really are unlimited and that is the case with Chiantis. You can pair it with food beyond traditional Italian servings, like grilled steaks, slow roasts or other meaty meals. All more reasons why people like to drink Italian wine.

Earlier it was mentioned that Italians can be innovative with their foods. The same is the case with wines. Italian winemakers take great pride in the fact that Italians have been making wine for thousands of years.

However, they also like the fact that they aren't constrained by historical wine production. Italian winemakers are continuously looking to find indigenous grapes from historical regions to make wines from, all in an attempt to contribute to a wide variety of enchanting, appealing, and unique flavors and tastes. Italian winemakers are usually progressive in nature and explore and produce beyond the boundaries for what is considered possible in wine.

There is no doubt that Italian wine is extremely food-friendly. Italian wine, however, has enough of its own character and make-up to be enjoyed on its own as well. Italian wine ages well because there's often a lot of tannin, fruit, and acidity involved, providing a good base and set of ingredients for aging. Those components will change in transformative ways to make even more flavors stand out, a result that can only come with the passage of time.

Anyone can find something they love in Italy. It is impossible to separate food, culture, and wine. In Italy, every region makes wine, often from grapes found nowhere else in the world, in a range of styles. And it's fundamentally tied to the food served in that region and thus, the true Italian culture that we admire, mimic, and want to be part of.

It has been said in many different ways but there is not a single doubt that wine plays an essential role in Italian culture.

These explanations for the popularity of Italian wines are many and varied. In truth, the popularity of Italian wines is due to the fact that regardless of region, they are consistently satisfying, and, almost without exception, over-deliver for the price, resulting in great value.

"Italian wine is the best" is clearly an opinion, but one held by millions of people around the world.

As any wine consumer considers their wine of choice, the important thing to remember is that wine is good if it tastes good to you. It is your choice, preference, and liking that matters. That's why people like and drink Italian wine.

Wine is more than just a drink in Italy. Italian wine is also more than just a drink for fans around the world. Wine is a very significant part of the Italian culture and almost always a must-have with food and at the dinner table.

Italians and visitors to the country drink wine at any time of day. They pay no attention to the time when drinking their wine. Many times, you can observe at lunch and even before and after lunch, people drinking wine. Want to know more about why people like to drink Italian wine? The next time you have the opportunity, just ask them.

TUSCANY PASSION

IN THE INTRODUCTION of this book, much was discussed regarding impressions, first thoughts, mind sets, and feelings about Italy. This continues with the Tuscany region of Italy.

It was also stated that this book is not a primer on Chianti wine or even Tuscany wines, per se. It is about the life surrounding the wines. Specifically, it is about the life, culture, and experiences of Tuscan inhabitants, families, workers, and especially Tuscan winemakers.

That life, that culture, those experiences begin and continue never-ending, with passion.

As Dianne Hales states in her best-selling book, *La Passione: How Italy Seduced the World*, these passions "...stem from an insatiable hunger to explore, discover, create, pursue beauty, feel deeply, love and live with every fiber of one's being."

While these are all related to Italy, it is these passions and thoughts that whisk our minds and thinking to the pinpointed location within Italy, of Tuscany. These are also the things people think of with just the mention of Tuscany.

In Tuscany, it's not only a passion around a consumed product but it's a passion around a way of life, a truly never-ending passion.

Italian passions may begin with thoughts or a desire, but they become more than what's in someone's mind. Italians and Italian afficionados have a great need to translate these visions into things: food, wine, art, history, culture, ideas, and more. Along with these visions and translations come behaviors, personalities, experiences, hopes, wishes, and dreams, for without these passions there would be no art, no culinary classics, no Italian way of life, and none of those things people think of when you mention Italy or Tuscany to them.

Historically, especially during the Renaissance period, passion has been part of the huge desire and pursuit for beauty, curiosity, and being.

When applying all of this to wine, it is more than just aromas and flavors—it's about people, conversation, and rich, engaging experiences.

The charm of Tuscany is based first on the rolling hills, lush landscapes, artistic cities, and quaint picturesque villages. If only this charm could speak, for it's the Italian and Tuscany traditions and legacy along with a huge cultural heritage, the extraordinary landscape and countryside that give it the character it is known for today.

For some, it's the Tuscan food that makes the region so exceptional; for others it is the juice of the grapes, the wines of Tuscany, the most famous being Chianti, produced in the area between Florence and Siena. Many will say that the sensory delights of robust food and tantalizing wines is the beating heart of Tuscan life, Tuscan people, and Italian culture.

While touring the Chianti regions of Greta and Castellina between Florence and Siena, there are "photo shoot" bus stops for visitors to enjoy all that the landscapes have to offer. Put the Tuscan sunset with this and you have the most picturesque Italian visual that will stay with you for a lifetime, representing Tuscany passion.

Italian passion is tangible. You can breathe the air that the many Renaissance artists and masters breathed. You can see and hear a winemaker sifting fistfuls of rich, fertile soil through his fingers as he spins his tales, stories, and heritage classics of those that came before him, his Italian forefathers.

As the Italian writer Luigi Barzini reflected in his classic *The Italians,* "The answer to what fills the soul, lies, at least in part, in the skies above and the earth below."

Earlier we talked about Italy being about the people, conversations, and rich, engaging experience, but it is more. It is about life, a lifestyle, a heritage, dreams of the future all fed by passion.

That's Italy. That's Tuscany.

Let's look more at the lifestyles that are backed by the ultimate of passion.

TRADITIONS

A S WE VISIT with each Tuscan winemaker, their heritage and family values quickly come into view. You can call it culture, customs, or traditions, but they are vivid throughout the region; the strong beliefs are carried from generation to generation. Traditions of Italy are sets of beliefs, values, and customs that are associated within the culture of Italian people. Many of these traditions have influenced Italian life for many, many centuries, and are still practiced in modern days. Usually, Italian traditions are directly related to Italian ancestors and the people, which tells us even more about Italian culture and history.

Before we generally define Italian traditions, let us first describe the basic categories and classifications where traditions fall.

While there are many, we will choose a few to focus on here: holidays, religion, food, and family. Many books are written about each of these individually. For now, we will approach in summary form.

We will focus on these to make the best portrayals, to characterize and to set the proper mood as we explore Tuscany winemakers and their traditions and lives.

Wikipedia defines a tradition as a belief or behavior passed down within a group or society with symbolic meaning or special significance with origins in the past. Wikipedia goes on to state that traditions can persist and evolve for thousands of years—the word tradition itself derives from the Latin "trader" literally meaning to transmit, to hand over, to give for safekeeping. As you read this, it's easy to think of Italian culture, traditions, and heritage.

Italian traditions are deep-rooted in the culture of its people and fulfill this definition of being handed over for safekeeping. Passed on by generation after generation, various traditions are sacred. Perhaps each generation makes a few changes—perhaps improvements, but the basic tradition usually stays intact.

We have already established that when someone mentions Italians many very clear images come to mind. This is because the Italian culture discussed above, is so widely known around the world that others' perception of it sometimes ends up being a stereotype or at least an animated visual in the mind. Italian culture, values, traditions, and beliefs are the pillars of the Italian society, no matter how you describe those subsets.

The Italian way of life is rich with tradition and culture. Traditional events and cultural activity range from weekly family get-togethers around the dinner table to extravagant holiday celebrations with joyful music, colorful decor, cultural dances, and of course, meals.

Here are just a few core truths of Italian culture that will serve as our base as the tradition conversation continues. Family is very, very important and it is at the core of all Italian life.

Italians hold elderly people in a position of respect, valuing their history and knowledge. People often rely on elders for help.

Social life in Italy revolves around meals.

The Italian work ethic is very important, and Italians have always been hard-working people. While ItalianPOD101.com states that Italians are well-known for their *"dolce far niente"* (pleasant idleness) and *"bella vita"* (good life) lifestyle, the importance of work for Italians is best expressed by the first article of the Italian Constitution which states: *"L'Italia è una repubblica democratica fondata sul lavoro."* (Italy is a democratic republic founded on work.)

Holidays

HOLIDAYS ARE AN important part of Italian culture, and they end up combining all of Italy's best cultural aspects.

Holidays are when families gather around special, traditional, and seasonal foods. Most holidays in Italy have a Catholic origin and these traditions are often honored in religious functions or rituals.

In Italian culture, holidays are the perfect "excuse" to bring out the best of the *Dolce Vita*, that particular way Italians enjoy life to its fullest. Italians usually celebrate all major holidays with family gathered around the table.

Italy's holidays include the familiar New Year's Day, Easter Monday, Labor Day (May 1), and Christmas Day, as well as others:

- Liberation Day—April 25

- Anniversary of the Founding of the Republic—June 2

- Feast of the Assumption or Ferragosto—August 15

- All Saints—November 1

- Feast of the Immaculate Conception—December 8

- St. Stephens Day—December 26

It is important to note that towns, cities, and villages in Italy celebrate the day of their own patron saint. These dates vary from location to location. For example, Rome celebrates the Feast of St. Paul and St. Peter on June 29.

"La Befana" is a typical Italian holiday. This is the Epiphany on January sixth, when an old and ugly lady on a flying broom brings candies to children.

Even without formal Italian holidays, Italians embrace any reason to get together with family.

While much has been written about Italian family traditions, family truly is at the core of Italian culture and traditions. Food, holidays, customs, traditions, and everyday life revolves around the institution of family and is central to the Italian culture and way of life.

Mention the phrase "big family" and many immediately think of Italian families. Italian families are devoted to the family institution and are very close, extending, many times, beyond the immediate family to all the other relatives from generation to generation. Grandparents often take care of their grandkids, and sons and daughters of Italian families live at home even if they've already started their professional careers.

People think Italians are argumentative by nature and by tradition. Much of this is due to the fact that Italian parents are very protective of their children, and they want to take care of anything and everything related to their children's education, work, finances, feelings, their own family lives, and upbringing. Even as adults, Italians involve parents in personal matters and in areas where parental advice is well spent.

Italians tend to act like families even at places of work. Things going on about town, community gossip, rumors, activities, all go on at once in an Italian place of work. Italians are very hard-working and have a very good work ethic. But they carry out their tasks with fun, in happy spirits, and by mixing work with pleasure (a common traditional theme heard over and over).

Most Italians are Roman Catholic. This isn't so surprising considering that Vatican City in Rome is the heart of Catholicism. In fact, Roman Catholics make up 90 percent of the population in Italy! Italians go to church regularly, where they pray and share their traditions.

Italy has long been the center of the Catholic world, since the day when Saint Peter settled in Rome and served as the first leader and bishop of the Catholic Church. The Vatican is here and the church has always had a direct or indirect influence over Italian life and politics (especially in the past).

One religious person of great influence among Italian spiritual leaders has been Saint Francis of Assisi, who is still often referred to as a role model for simple living and harmony with nature. As we learn more about culture and traditions, this living model is consistent with all that we see and experience in Tuscany.

The magnificence and influence of the Catholic Church are evident in all of the beauty and number of churches, cathedrals, and domes which are seen everywhere, from larger cities to small Tuscan villages. Philosophers and scientists that we read so much about have populated the region since ancient times, through the Middle Ages and Renaissance mostly due to the cultural power of the Catholic Church.

In Italian culture, families socialize and celebrate often. Even on a regular day, they'll meet in each other's homes for dinner or head to restaurants together. Food equals love and tradition in Italian culture. Italy is home to the simplest, traditional home cuisine.

In Italy, food is at the center of celebrations and family gatherings. In the past, the most important meal was "*il pranzo*" (lunch). It's still common for families to get together around a table on Sundays to celebrate "*il pranzo della domenica*" (Sunday's lunch) with the typical succession of "*antipasto, primo, secondo, contorno, frutta, dolce e caffè*" (appetizer, first course, second course, side dish, fruit, dessert, and coffee).

Meals on special occasions can go on for hours. Eating is not just about food and nourishment, but rather about pleasure, indulgence, and being with loved ones to share in each other's joys.

Italians are extremely proud of their gastronomy, and every region, city, and village boasts its unique cuisine. Flavors and traditional preparation methods are very important; Italians try as much as possible to preserve and protect their culinary products.

It's hard not to love Italian cuisine. Every region has its own distinctive and memorable flavors that come from that region's Italian customs, culture, and family traditions. It's a pure treat for the senses. By tradition, if you want an Italian lunch, you usually won't have it served to you until 1:00 pm and dinner most often takes place at or after 8:00 pm. There are no senior early bird specials or "linner" servings.

Italian food menu items usually feature courses such as antipasto, primo, secondo, contorno, and dolce. On any ordinary day when dining with Italians, most people will only choose primo which is either pasta-based and a secondo which contains meat or fish. Depending on their order, they may also go with a contorno, which is a side dish. Salad is sometimes optional and served later in the meal.

Each of the different geographical regions within Italy has a different traditional style of cuisine, based on what is readily available in that area. For example, coastal regions are often known for their seafood dishes.

Central Italy favors olive oils and cheese. Beef and wild boar are readily available and used frequently, along with cured meats. Stuffed pasta is famous in this region.

Southern Italian cuisine traditionally involves tomato sauces and olive oil. Citrus fruit is also a popular ingredient in the south. Southern Italy is famous for the world's first opened pizzeria in Naples.

Northern Italian cuisine does not include olive oil as frequently as southern Italian cuisine, and rice is generally preferred to pasta as the starch in dishes. You may notice them labeled as risotto and polenta. Rather than using tomato sauce, cream-based sauces are more prevalent.

Are these really traditions or just regional fare? Looking back over time and into history and following the food evolution map, you will see that these truly are traditional in nature and carry on to today's time.

A couple of other traditional food points are that cappuccino is not the first drink of choice after a heavy Italian meal. Milk with a meal is not something you see and since cappuccino has plenty of milk in it, it's not something Italians order after dinner. Secondly, since Italians prize the fresh fish and shellfish from the sea, they intend that you enjoy its many sensations. For this reason, you will never see Italians putting grated cheese or sprinkling parmesan on top of any seafood or fish dish like the heavy cheese graters in other parts of the world.

Now that you know more about Italian traditions and culture, are you hungry? Are you thirsty? Do you just want to get your family together for a monumental event? Do you want to tell stories of your past relatives? If not, there will be many more stories and items of interest to make sure that happens and to continue touching your senses.

Tuscany Thoughts

CONSIDER THE THINGS Italy is famous for: food, cooking, art, history, political factions and wars between territories, religion, family, and more. We have already discussed some of these and will continue to. Regardless of what is famous you can bet that Italians approach their lives and heritage with great pride, vitality, and most of all, passion!

There is a French phrase often used, Joie de vivre," which interpreted in English means to express cheerful enjoyment of life, an exultation of spirit. It can be a joy of conversation, joy of eating, joy of drinking wine, and joy of anything and everything that an Italian might do. It's a philosophy of and approach to life.

That's the passion of Italians!

On a recent trip to Florence, a street marketer advised me to inhale deeply the same air that Da Vinci and Michelangelo breathed. Even in Tuscany vineyards, winemakers will sift through the sandy soil and tell you that it's the same soil that grew the wines of their ancestors and forefathers. That, too, is Italian passion.

Wine is about more than just tastings, bouquets, flavors, and pairings. Wine, especially Italian wine, is about the people you drink with, the conversation, the aromas, and flavors all producing the most passionate, appealing, and pleasing experiences. At the top of that list is Tuscany, a wine region unlike anywhere else in the world. Call it a mystique; call it a lifestyle; call it Italian passion.

When someone mentions or you think about Italy, many, many things come to mind. I could attempt to list them (and I will here, albeit briefly) but surely the list will be different for others. Of course, I'll be biased here with the order of thoughts but only for the first few. After all, personal preferences guide all of our thoughts and passions.

Here we go—Italian Thoughts and Passions:

- Wine

- Food: pizza, pasta (and way more)

- Gelato

- Rolling hills

- Art: paintings and sculpture

- Fast cars

- History

- Culture

- Architecture

- Music

- Fashion

- Language

While these are all related to Italy, it is these passions and thoughts that whisk one to the pinpointed location within Italy of Tuscany.

There is no mistake that the first on this list is wine. In Italy, in Tuscany in particular, it's not only a consumed product but it's a life. It's that life that is a starting, middle, and ending point here, although it truly is never ending.

Dianne Hales is truly the predominant maestra of Italian passion: "Without passion, there would be no literature, no art, no music, no romance, perhaps none of the wonders Italians have wrought.

The Renaissance extended the definition of la passione to an all-consuming dedication to a worthy pursuit, most often beauty in its infinite variety."

Even for those without Italian heritage, a Tuscan visit just feels like coming to and belonging to home.

Let's look deeper into passion.

ITALIAN CHIANTI HAS ITS OWN STORY

I TALY IS MADE up of sensory overload, whether for the eyes, the taste buds, the aromas, or the many memories, once there. Imagine visiting one of their fabled sites, exiting, and then taking in an early lunch at a corner cucina, its few tables, seating about 12 people, covered with red and white checkered tablecloths. That is one of my truly memorable experiences when visiting Tuscany.

The experience was further added to when two elderly Italian natives entered for their early lunch, late morning routine: lunch, conversation, bonding, storytelling, and wine. I am offering the utmost of respect by calling these two compatriots elderly. As a matter of fact, they were octogenarians in full vitality.

The sequence of events was first, an order of the local wine. Upon further investigation and observation, it was clearly the local Chianti. After all we were in Tuscany.

The first round of storytelling corresponded to the first bottle of wine. Following this was another bottle of the local Chianti and a pizza. Although pizza is not native fare to Italians, it was that day, in that place with these two. Pizza was followed by an entrée which appeared to be lasagna-like. The scent of basil, oregano, spice, tomatoes, beef, pork, and veal all on top of a heaping helping of steamy pasta filled the air.

The stories did not stop amongst the act of eating and imbibing. Following this was a salad and more Chianti.

When asking our new friends, the octogenarians, to share with us what they were tasting and/or experiencing with their Chianti, they described it as an earthy, rustic, wine that is high in tannins (they mentioned mouth drying characteristics). They did mentions tones of fruit, cherries, plums, and strawberries, much like many tasters of Chianti mention. We have heard of smokiness as well. Many would mention a medium-bodied wine. All of these taste elements suggest that this wine goes with just about any food being craved at the moment. Just ask our octogenarians. Whether it's their pizza, their tomato sauce covered pasta or their salads, Chianti pairs well. Period. Even as grilled meats and Italian salami enter the meal scene, Chianti pairing still prevails.

It's almost as if no Italian meal is complete without a glass of the ruby red staple, flowing throughout the meal. That ruby red staple is Chianti. We are not talking about the short, non-standard, straw-covered bottle you might associate with Tuscany wines but a staple that is very approachable, enjoyable, and therefore memorable.

The straw covered bottle that the name Chianti connotes is called a "fiasco." This innovation was originally intended to keep the bottles upright and steady during loud parties and celebrations as well as provide protection during hauling and shipping. The Chianti wine enjoyed by those two octogenarians refers to the region of Tuscany where Chianti wine comes from, not the grape itself.

Throughout its history, Chianti in these fiascos was enjoyed at the dinner tables of peasants, commoners, noblemen, and popes alike. The great scientist, Galileo Galilei, had admirable words for the wine in the flask: "These traditional bottles can be unadorned and little presentable but can contain an excellent wine—glorious and divine."

Merriam-Webster defines staple, and it's so appropriate here, as something that is used, needed, or enjoyed constantly, usually by many individuals. Chianti conforms to this definition in Italy as well as worldwide when it comes to wine consumption.

That's the essence of Chianti; that's the essence that can touch the soul.

We have mentioned thoughts that come to mind when asking wine lovers and even visitors about Italy and Italian wine. Chianti is the wine of note for many. This may be because Chianti is the most consumed wine in Italy and the most consumed Italian wine all over the world. Chianti is representative and characteristic of what Italy means to the world of wine and its many consumers.

Why are we separating out Chianti here to talk about? Since the Tuscany region is best known for Chianti, it deserves its own story and review. Here we review the wine, the grapes, the end products and the wineries involved.

Some of the wineries we visited are heavy into Chianti production; others produce Italian wines other than Chianti.

Let's give Chianti its proper mention, attention, and citation.

A Chianti is any wine produced in the Chianti region of central Tuscany.

The wine region known as Chianti is settled by Florence to its north and Siena to its south. The region is full of Italian beauty, culture, and tradition. The landscapes are widely known as backdrops in Renaissance paintings. Throughout the region there is an abundance of old-world castles, timeless chapels, the many bell towers, countryside farmhouses, hills, olive groves, and the almost countless vineyards. It is a genuine place which was the origination to the wine known by the region's name both locally and worldwide, Chianti.

In the book, *Chianti Classico: The Search for Tuscany's Noblest Wine,* authors Bill Nesto and Frances Di Savino ask the over-arching question, "What is Chianti?" Many wine consumers are often confused about whether Chianti is a grape or a region. The answer is that it is both. The question that Nesto and Di Savino pose is how the Chianti region should be defined and what wines should therefore receive the Chianti designation.

Chianti has been at the heart of several regional Italian wars including one in the Middle Ages between Florence and Siena and another between the interests of Chianti Classico and those of the region just outside of Chianti.

Also, historically speaking, in the mid to late 19th century, Baron Bettino Ricasoli (later Prime Minister of the Kingdom of Italy) helped establish Sangiovese as the blend's dominant grape, creating the requirement for today's Chianti wines. Chianti is a deep ruby, red wine that comes from these described areas and origins of Tuscany but can contain grapes of other origins during processing and blending. One exception to this is the wine known as Chianti Classico. This must be solely made from red Sangiovese grapes.

The original area dictated by the decree of Cosimo III de' Medici of the famed Medici family would eventually be considered the heart of the modern "Chianti Classico" subregion.

Even in later times, Chianti has made other historical appearances. There was an occasion after the first self-sustaining nuclear chain reaction, on December 2, 1942, when physicist Enrico Fermi opened a bottle of Chianti to make a toast. The bottle's straw wrapper was signed by the 49 people who witnessed the historical event in an abandoned rackets court beneath the University of Chicago's old football stadium in Illinois. Most of the signatures from then have faded, but a few remain, including Fermi's, written just below the bottle's label.

Since the wine here refers to the region of Tuscany where Chianti wine comes from, it is worth noting the area.

Navigating the countryside between the cities of Florence and Siena, the predominant Chianti region, reveals what has been described as a majestic landscape. This landscape is further described as one having narrow country roads, hillsides consumed by forests, and vineyards up and down the landscape slopes. Sprinkle this with medieval castles, Romanesque chapels, and grand forestations and you have what could be the scenery in the background of a famous Renaissance painting.

It is with this history, this tradition, this legacy that Chianti continues to capture its place on top of the Italian wine pedestal and in many cases, the world pedestal.

As Wikipedia states, Francesco Redi, an Italian physician, naturalist, biologist, and poet referred to as the "founder of experimental biology," and as the "father of modern parasitology" in the early 17th century stated that, "Good Chianti, that aged, majestic and proud wine, enlivens my heart, and frees it painlessly from all fatigue and sadness."

Here's to all those with good hearts reading this and those that want a better heart or soul!

THE BLACK ROOSTER LEGEND

B EFORE DIVING DEEP into the lives of Tuscan vintners, let's take a look at a little Tuscan wine symbolism. That symbol is the Black Rooster.

I'm going to cut right to the chase revealing the star subject here: Every bottle of Chianti Classico is marked with a black rooster.

When Chianti Classico wines are talked about, the Black Rooster always makes an appearance in conversation. The Black Rooster proudly shows itself on the neck of every bottle of true Chianti Classico wines. But why a black rooster? What's the story of the rooster? Like all good stories there is usually a legend behind them, especially in this case, and the legend gave birth to the symbol.

The Gallo Nero (Black Rooster) was the historic symbol of the League of Chianti. Since then, the Black Rooster has become the notable symbol of the wines of Chianti Classico. The legend dates back to the period of the League of Chianti of 1384. During this time there were clearly open hostilities and out and out wars between The Republic of Florence and The Republic of Siena for control of what was then known as the Chianti territory.

The Republic of Florence and The Republic of Siena in medieval times were relentlessly dealing with a longstanding provincial land dispute and bloody wars, where each one of them wanted larger and more generous border areas for their regions.

The two republics—historical enemies—competed for supremacy over the Chianti region, which was considered a valuable, strategic area of Tuscany. It was strategic because of the proximity and positioning between the two cities.

The two rival cities bargained and bickered and still could not agree on where the border should be to determine who would control Chianti. They did, finally, however, come up with a feud-ending solution that would avoid bloodshed (somewhat amazing for that usually combative time period).

To end this long-standing dispute and establish future legal borders, both the cities came

up with an unusual idea to establish the new
legal, remapped borders of their territories to
include respective portions of the territory Chianti. Simply stated, (simply stated now but not
necessarily in medieval times) on a specified
day, two horsemen would each ride off from
their respective hometowns at the first light of
day, one from Florence and one from Siena, towards one another. Where the two met would
be the newly established legal border between
the two republics.

One challenge, however, remained for each
rider. In the 14th century there were no alarm
clocks to alert anyone to a specified time of
awakening. Aside from remaining sleepless
through the night before, the riders had to de-
vise a way to be alerted to a wake-up time.

The only alarm clock available in the day to
wake up the riders was the rooster and its early
morning crowing.

The Sienese people chose a white rooster to wake their rider up at dawn. During the
days before the event, they treated the bird to
all possible rooster and cage comforts, fed him
well, raised him silky and lustrous, not to mention fat and plump, with the idea that it would
loudly crow to wake their rider at dawn wanting
more of this grand treatment. They overlooked
the fact that a full stomach could make him le-
thargic.

The Florentines put their black rooster in an uncomfortable cage, provided no animal luxuries and starved the bird for several days before the event. Their thoughts were that this would make the rooster wake up earlier in search of more food and water. As we all know after any gorge, our full stomach contributes to a lazy day. A starving stomach tends to keep you awake, drives you to search for food, and in this case crow violently for you to feed it; an alarm clock surely to go off earlier than a complacent, happy rooster.

That approach worked for Florence. On the day of the event, the Florentine black rooster, desperately starved and cooped up in an unforgiving cage, started crowing before the break of day. The Florentine rider saddled up and took off with a definite head start, much earlier than the opposing rider from Siena. The fat, plump, well-fed rooster was relaxed, and complacent, crowing long after dawn had broken, and much later than the black rooster of Florence. The rider from Siena couldn't fill the gap of time between him and his opposing rider from Florence.

With the earlier start, the Florentine rider dominated the contest and claimed much more of the Chianti territory than the Siena rider. Distances vary, but some say the Sienese rider was less than 12 kilometers, (7.5 miles) into his ride when the Florentine met up with him in a locality called Fonterutoli. This was after the rider from Florence had galloped for more than 100 kilometers (62 miles)!

That's the legend of the Chianti Classico Black Rooster. The rooster was adopted as an official emblem by the League of Chianti in 1384. The next time you shop, buy, or see a bottle of Chianti, look for the fabled rooster. You will then know the story behind the Black Rooster symbol.

WINEMAKING AS A CAREER/VOCATION

SINCE WE ARE here to learn about the lives of Tuscan winemakers, let's look at the career itself.

Where else can you find a vocation where you can take a raw material, in this case grapes, make a highly desirable and enjoyable product, and then sell that product directly to the consumer? Winemaking allows that to happen.

Charting a course in the wine industry gives you the potential to branch out into a multitude of areas within the same industry. Those interested start learning about wine, the drink of enjoyment for many, and the process to get to that finished product. The interest to get answers to the "what and how" leads one down a winemaking path and maybe on the way to owning a vineyard, a winery, a branding and bottling operation, or some other facet of the industry. This desire is the start.

There are those that get started because they come from a wine-producing family or have relatives that want them to carry on the heritage and traditions that are deep rooted in their lifestyle. The country and region has great potential in winemaking due to the fact that each region has its own unique heritage, history, traditions, and culture, as well as many local grape varieties per region.

Regardless it still comes back to that high level of desire to learn the basics and take them further.

The mere thought of working in the wine industry conjures of thoughts of hiking through tranquil vineyards and experiencing nature through the vines and vegetation. Add that desire to the rest of the above and you have the perfect career choice and potential path for you to fulfill that desire.

So what does a winemaker do? What are the activities of a vintner?

As you will hear from those interviewed in this book almost without exception, being a winemaker involves many different activities with no day being the same as the day before or after. It will be a recurring theme as each winemaker is interviewed. The vocation of winemaking requires knowledge of many related things. It is more than turning grapes into wine. It is all the activity between the growing of the grapes to the bottling and distribution of the finished product. All of this different activity makes the day-to-day activities in the area of winemaking different from wine professional to wine professional.

According to Nova Cadamatre in a blog she wrote for the Wine & Spirit Education Trust, "Winemakers are in charge of the decisions of when to pick the grapes, what yeasts to use, what style of wine will be made, how that wine will be aged, for how long it will be aged, and any blending decisions which may need to be made to perfect the final wine. Some winemakers may only be focused on preparing wines for bottling while others, for example, may be in charge of taking care of bulk wine to sell to external customers who will then bottle it on their own."

She goes on to state that, "Many winemakers oversee the entire winemaking process from grapes to bottle. Depending on the size of the winery, a winemaker's job can vary widely. At a small winery they can be the person actually pulling hoses and getting dirty whereas at a large winery there may be a team of winemakers who are issuing directions to a large group of cellar workers."

Today you will also find many winemakers involved in the marketing of their brands, public relations, consumer relations, and more marketing activity after the wine is produced.

Because of the many different activities and opportunities to solve problems within the winery and the winemaking process, many will say that one of the more important qualities that a winemaker can possess is creativity.

Some will say that winemaking is an art. Some will say it's a science. Regardless, putting creativity to work during the operation and process has become a critical skill of a successful winemaker. Good winemakers work with their lands and the natural elements (weather and soil) to pull the wine to its maximum potential. This then translates into wines that reflect the winemaker, their surroundings, origins, and heritage, resulting in a wine's own personality.

In all of the interviews with Tuscan winemakers, many common characteristics and resounding themes immediately surface. In a nutshell, these are a desire for knowledge, curiosity, a deep-down desire to create great wine for others to enjoy, and pushing to get to the next level of quality or something unique and talked about. We heard "continuing education and continuing improvement" talked about at each step of our journey.

I know just what you are thinking right now. That sounds so romantic, like a dream job and one that glides from day to day, from bottle to bottle. Let me stop you there. It is hardly all romance and hardly smooth gliding every step of the way. Add to this dash of romance the cleaning of tanks, vats, equipment and barrels, hot and cold days, early and late, muddy vineyards, malfunctioning process components, and process hiccups. These things need to be dealt with as a winemaker can't ditch the product in process and start over. There are cycles to tend with whether process related, weather related, or people related. All of this means a lot of hard work and investment in equipment. Accepting this makes winemaking a rewarding career and the choice of many whether as part of an upbringing or a conscious choice for future endeavors.

If you want to become a winemaker, you must love the business, participate in the fields, vineyards, and harvest, and get your hands dirty, literally. You need to understand grapes and feel their evolution from start to finish, from the vine to the bottle.

That is what we found in those that we interviewed as you read about winemaking as a career, here.

GENERALLY SPEAKING—A DAY IN THE LIFE

A S WE VISIT with each winemaker and winery, we make a lot of observations and try to dispel myths and find the real story of what a typical Tuscan winemaker does and how they live. It begs the question, what do people think a winemaker does.

A lot of people think that these winemakers sit around while sniffing and drinking wine at all hours of the day. They envision swirling, cheese and meat trays, and a life of entertainment and celebration.

Some envision the winemaker ambling and walking through his vine-covered land, a rolling green landscape under the Tuscan sun.

If only a winemaker's job and life were this romantic. If only all this was true. If only that was the definition of a winemaker's work.

In actuality, these things do exist, but it is only a very small, with an emphasis on very small, sliver of life and work.

What Do You Really Do?

WHAT DO WINEMAKERS really do? We are about to learn about a lot of activity from several winemakers.

Yes, as we are about to learn throughout this book, winemakers do spend days smelling and drinking wine. After all, they are responsible for the wine meeting taste, blending, and quality goals. In order for this to happen the winemaker needs to understand what parts of the process influence grapes and eventual wine to meet their quality standards. This entails monitoring weather patterns, soil conditions, and more. A lot of the job is scheduling and planning oriented. Equipment maintenance must be tended to and watched over. Crews to process, blend, and bottle must be in place. Labs and testing must take place and be supervised. These too, are the responsibility of the winemaker. All a lot different than smelling, swirling, tasting, and drinking!

Once in the bottle, the winemaker's job turns into event planning, PR, marketing, distribution, and sales. Entertaining and educating consumers is a part of this. These things drive the winemaker towards his life goals and ensures ongoing harvests, seasons, and production.

We will generally look at this day in the life of the winemaker and later look at real life activity of actual winemakers at specific Tuscan wineries.

Generally speaking, a winemaker's work is keyed into the harvest: Activity is split between pre-harvest, harvest, and post-harvest times. Duties are further broken down between morning and later in the day, cool times and hot times, vineyard time and cellar time, all followed by office time.

That seems to be the breakdown of activity for each winemaker. Sure, there are exceptions and differences, but we will wait until the reviews of specific winemakers to understand this fully.

During harvest, the winemaker spends his morning time, when it is cooler, in the vineyard. Believe it or not, grapes heat up as the day gets warmer and can yield different taste properties and analysis (grapes, straight off the vine before winemaking) depending on temperature. The winemaker then tastes grape after grape after grape, all in an effort to gauge the grape's growing, maturation, and ripening progression. It is at this point that, under the direction of the winemaker, the decision to pick or not to pick happens. Sometimes it is ready at this tasting point to pick and harvest and sometimes the winemaker decides the grapes need to stay on the vine to accumulate more sugar and flavors. This process could consume up to half of a day's work or a few hours. Of the thousands of grapes tasted, the winemaker knows through his education, experience, and expertise, the stage of each grape. Now that's an amazing wine-tasting palate. Once tasted, it's then off to the cellar for the "inside" work as the day is starting to warm up.

At this point the tasting is not done. Wines, at various stages of the winemaking process, are tasted to check fermentation and the flavors to eventually determine which wines will be finalized and bottled within its respective appellation/label. After a couple hours of cellar work, it's time to plan activity: more harvesting schedules, bottling, and eventual shipping logistics. Of course, planning for all the people involved in this is up to the chief winemaker.

Finally towards the end of the day, the winemaker is back at his office reviewing all the day's activity, lab results and analyses, adjustments in process needs, and planning the next day's work. The ending point of the day is dependent on the winemaker's desire, work ethic, family life outside the winery, customer engagement, and more. There are workaholics and there are those who are master delegators, literally enjoying the fruits of all the labor.

This is an overview of daily activity; more detail is to come from specific winemakers interviewed. Everyone is different in one respect or another. There are, however, commonalities among all.

Throughout anything involved in Italian winemaking or Italian life in general, we discuss passion. Passion and work translate into a labor of love. That is common with everyone we encountered who is involved in winemaking.

Another common element is that wine production is a business. Expenses must be managed whether it's on capital-intensive equipment, sales and marketing, distribution, or the people who make it all happen. While there are good days and bad days and times of elation and times of frustration, almost all winemakers told us that this all has to be kept in the proper perspective. They fully realize they are furthering their own passions, their own family legacies, and enjoyment for them and the consumers of their wines.

While we reviewed the day in the life and the activity of a Tuscan winemaker, let's look at the people side of that. Specifically, what personal qualities and characteristics come out for each and every winemaker?

You will read, and we heard over and over, things related personally to zest for the job, passion, passion, and more passion, drive, innovation, and a goal of legacy.

CAMPOCHIARENTI

A VISIT TO SAN Gimignano near Siena, Italy takes you to the Campochiarenti Winery also known as Azienda Agricola Campochiarenti. Campochiarenti is known best as a boutique winery of Tuscany.

The actual location is situated in an old village along Francigena road between Poggibonsi and San Gimignano, in the Chianti Colli Senesi region in the Tuscan hills. The winery is just east of San Gimignano very close to Siena, facing the Chianti Classico district.

This winemaking area, in the thick of Tuscany, has historical importance for wine production as there is documentation of wine production and delivery from the Campochiarenti region from as far back as the late 1200s. The winery that stands now was established in 1977 by the current owners, the Rosti family, to acknowledge and continue the rich history of Campochiarenti.

Daniele Rosti is the current owner, son of founding owner Gian Ambrogio Rosti. Daniele oversees complete production of the quality wines from this estate. His insight, knowledge, and passion come out loud and clear when learning about his vineyard, process, philosophies, and history.

His story starts with learning about his path to Tuscany.

There are many different stories about how people got to Tuscany. Some were born and bred there and have never left. Some have moved around Italy and back again. Others have moved around the world only to return to their roots. Daniele Rosti falls into the middle category of residents.

Also as with many, it is the family unit or extended family that influences the travels and eventual return. That was the case of Daniele Rosti and his family. His pathway to Tuscany was led by his father, Gian Ambrogio Rosti.

Characteristic of Italian families, there is a strong bond between father and son. To a young boy, his father is a titan from whose shoulders you can see the world and beyond. Fathers have a strong role, function, and responsibility in Italian families. It is often said that Italian fathers are the "soul of the house."

The Rosti family was originally from Tuscany. They later moved to Milan. In fact, Milan is the birthplace of our featured winemaker here, Daniele Rosti. In 1977, the Rosti family returned from Milan to Tuscany and assumed ownership of Campochiarenti.

Daniele's father was a successful doctor. Upon his return to Tuscany, Gian Ambrogio Rosti was known as a simple man working long hours in a day in dirty, hot, dusty vineyards. It is of this work ethic that father Gian taught his son the many lessons of faith and hard work, all by his daily life examples.

The property the Rosti family acquired had been a monastery for the church of St. Nicholas dating back to the end of the 10th century.

History of St. Nicholas Church

The Campochiarenti history begins at the end of the 10th century when the Church of Saint Nicholas was built. This church is named in official documents signed by Pope Alessandro II in 1070. The power of the owners, this church, and village had become more important because of the alliance with San Gimignano which was fighting against Poggibonsi at a time where there were frequent battles between adjacent cities.

As the Bishop domain on San Gimignano was completed, the area of San Gimignano needed loans from the notable bankers of Florence. In the mid 14th century, the San Gimignano area became part of the domain of Florence. This was reaffirmed in later years with additional pontificals (official Papal documents) signed by the popes in office.

Vernaccia and other vintage wines have been exported from Campochiarenti and surrounding areas since 1276. Vernaccia is the most important wine in the history of Tuscany because it has maintained the same variety and quality characteristics over the centuries.

The church and the convent in Campochiarenti show the importance of this place and how the agricultural production of olives and grapes has been done during the last 1,000 years.

In 1977, new ownership started the renewal of the vineyards and the buildings to restore the prominence and importance of the area.

As the family took over, restoration started with a focus not only on buildings but on the planting of new vines more conducive to the climatic conditions of the San Gimignano area.

The immediate attention included the restoration of the Chapel attached to the former Monastery, which still stands today as a symbol of Tuscan glory.

Daniele Rosti now calls this home. As you will learn here, he is involved in all aspects of winemaking from vineyard management to product management and marketing, and all that goes into delivering a quality Tuscany wine product to the ultimate consumer.

The Rosti family, for at least three to four generations back, were always involved in farming. This included their time in Milan. Cows and milk were the products of their farming. Dr. Rosti decided to follow the passion of wine growing and winemaking in his native land. Daniele likens this farming and milk production to now, his winemaking in Tuscany. He associates winemaking as the "milk of the cellar."

The family's desire was to continue the growing and farming activity in Tuscany while sending their philosophy around the world. That philosophy, simply stated, was based on the respect of nature. Daniele states that, "... we live in nature, we work in nature, and we want to preserve nature for future generations." He goes on to say, "We want to do our best to preserve soil and earth in the best way possible using the healthiest and most eco friendly techniques available." He is quick to point out there are no poisons used on the ground or soil in their winemaking. Chemical treatment is reduced to minimal levels to produce wine. As another example, the olive oil produced in the off wine-season is produced using only soil, rain, and hand work.

As far as quality goes, Daniele will tell you that the main factor in determining quality is growing top quality fruit. The production philosophy of Campochiarenti is that quality grows in the vineyard. Therefore, work in the field is essential to produce excellent wines. The growth of the vines is strictly related to the climate, to the water availability, to the sun, and to the chemical elements available in the soil that feeds the vines. All the weeds are mechanically or manually removed. The soil is naturally balanced without using chemicals or poisons. If something is not in the soil then it cannot be in the grapes, and therefore not in the wine. The wine produced is healthier and more natural.

The key word here is NATURAL. The wines are made as naturally as possible with minimum intervention in the vineyard and with the winemaking.

Daniele believes for the best grapes it's important to minimize the effect of any products used. It's about using the 1,000 years of experience of many generations with these ancient varieties for the best results. Campochiarenti's approach is based on the ancestral rural wisdom, joined to modern scientific research, to obtain grapes with traditional flavors.

Let's take a look at the actual activities of this winemaker's day, his challenges, and more insight to bring out even more richness of Tuscany and its fine wines.

When asking Daniele what his typical day consists of, he tells us what many Tuscany winemakers state and that is every day is different. The different days are sometimes made up of standard winemaking production tasks; other times it's solving problems. There are always situations that pop up that require attention and time from the winemaker. He truly does have a plan as to what the day's activities should consist of.

He states, in summary fashion, that his day and his activity is "to control the vineyard and to check what happens in the cellar." He does this himself along with his personally chosen staff that reports to him. Internal communication here is a very important part of his activity as well as assigning jobs and tasks. There is detailed training involved as well as traditional management like any other business.

Controlling the vineyard takes on tasks of pruning which Daniele is quick to point out is one of the most, if not the most, important tasks outside of the cellar.

From the beginning of the spring season as nature has taken its course, and during grape growing, Daniele checks the quality of the crop of grapes, which, to him, defines the next step of growing, the eventual harvest, and the next steps of the process. Nature helps him prepare for a healthy vine and grape growth along the way.

At harvest time, his time is spent managing the picking of the grapes. It is at this point that many things in winemaking take place simultaneously, requiring a sharp mind, keen eye, and multitasked management of people, the process, and product.

Of course, daily activities do not come without their sets of challenges. It's late August and the harvest of the current crop of grapes is just starting. Yields are affected by overly hot weather and animal damage, especially from deer. The winery is at the mercy of these as they are somewhat out of the control of the winemaker.

While this captures the winemaking process, in Daniele's situation as the owner/chief winemaker, one fourth to one third of his time is spent on paperwork and Italian bureaucracy which he considers time away from winemaking and with due respect for the necessity of it, almost a waste of time.

All of this work—from mornings walking the vineyard to the mundane task of paperwork—result in a quality wine and a way of life that realizes the dreams of Daniele's father, Gian.

To honor his father, Daniele created the S Cuvée, GianAmbrogio IGT (Typical Geographic Indication) Toscana Rosso 2008 "GAR".

The wine is dedicated to his late father with the Latin phrase spoken by his father on the label of each bottle:

> *"Est modus in rebus*
> *Sunt certi denique fines*
> *Quos ultra citraque*
> *Nequit consistere rectum."*

The translation advises moderation in all things, the ends of which cannot abide or be accepted. John Fodera, Founder and writer of *Tuscan Vines*, the leading authority on Tuscan and Italian wine in the U.S., focusing on Italian wine and recipes that honor the Italian culture, offers his interpretation of the Rosti Latin motto as, "There is meaning in things and there are limits that we cannot go beyond; but we must consist of steadfast devotion."

Pure and simple, Daniele Rosti states that this motto exemplifies living in the right way, respecting limits that nature gives us, and always trying to do better.

In wrapping up with Daniele Rosti, his personality is best characterized by what is *stated as part of his message to consumers:*

"In our wines you can feel not only the tradition of Tuscany but also our feelings, our values, the respect for Nature and the love for the vines, that our family taught us. If you have the same love, you are ready for tasting."

Italian Wine Bureaucracy

SINCE DANIELE MENTIONED it and can actually talk at length about it, let's take a brief look at Italian wine bureaucracy.

It truly is a fact and not just a prevailing opinion that Italian wine bureaucracy is a necessary evil and something that takes up the time of every winemaker and winery owner. Everything Italian has a multitude of positive, descriptive adjectives ranging from beauty, appealing to the senses and positive experiences. That is until a Tuscan winemaker has to deal with taxes and bureaucracy. When asking various winemakers about their daily duties almost all of them relate the whole winemaking process and end up on the time consuming, painful process of Italian wine bureaucracy.

Italy's hundreds of thousands of vineyards are subject to strict legal rules and regulations known as *Disciplinari di Produzione*.

Like most everything in Italy, the idea of rules governing wine production and bureaucracy is as old as the winery estates themselves. Under Roman rule in 154 BC, it was illegal to grow grapes beyond the Alps. This put undue pressure on the thirsty inhabitants of Gaul, forcing them to send more and more slaves to Rome and surrounding Italian regions in exchange for Italian wine.

John Mariani, contributor to *Forbes*, reported that the Italian wine industry in 1963, under the laws of the European Union, had to identify and classify its wine grapes and regions, causing the Italian Ministry of Agriculture to create two designations for labels: D.O.C. (denominazione d'origine controllata: a denomination of controlled origin) and D.O.C.G., in which the "G" stood for "garantita" (guarantee). He went on to report that it was a bureaucratic attempt to make sense of the maverick way Italians grew grapes and made wine, and it forced vintners to adhere to strict rules about which grapes must be used to make a particular regional wine like Chianti in Tuscany.

A thesis by John Lisman, for the Washington Research Library Consortium (WRLC) and entitled *The Italian Wine Industry: Progress and Lessons* states:

"The *Disciplinare di Produzione* were strict guidelines regulating any number of characteristics of wine including the geographic area of production, alcohol content, grape varietals used for the wine, percentages of varietals that could be blended, vineyard and grape yields, and even labeling and aging requirements. These strict government regulations aimed to protect the great tradition of terroir and ensure consistency and high standards in any Italian wine awarded an appellation."

The strict regulations often hold winemakers back from experimentation which would yield an equally good, if not better, wine without the regulations.

The laws, rules, regulations, reporting procedures, and bureaucracy attempts to establish controls as to the quality of the Italian wine that is put in the bottle. It's time consuming but a necessary evil and something often talked about with a true winery owner and operator. The bureaucracy has been in place for a long time and will probably exist for a longer time into the future. That is just the Italian way, especially as it relates to wine.

Passione Divina

THERE IS ONE good story coming out of Campochiarenti that makes it different from all the Tuscan wineries written about here and that you will read about or visit. It is a result of Daniele Rosti always trying to improve, to make things better, to try new things, despite the bureaucracy in place.

Campochiarenti offers the wine labeled Passione Divina. This is one truly unique Tuscan wine. If you were told about two families, one wine and one passion all made into one, this wine would be it.

Passione Divina is the first wine ever produced by two wineries located in Italy and the USA. Of course, Azienda Agricola Campochiarenti is the Italian counterpart and, as we know now, is located in San Gimignano (Siena) Italy. Rabbit Ridge Winery is the American counterpart, located in Paso Robles, California.

Passione Divina means Divine Passion. Passion is all over anything and everything related to Tuscan wines. The name expresses the idea behind this wine: Create a wine that shares a common passion for the respective countries, Italy and the USA, the vineyards, and traditions.

The blend is unique: 70% of the grapes are from Tuscany (Italy) and 30% are from Paso Robles (CA). According to Daniele, every variety is produced separately, with the blending done only before finalizing the bottling in Paso Robles, California.

You will not find this type of venture with any other two wineries in the USA or in Italy; it truly is a singular venture that stands out amongst both wineries and both wine markets. This venture is best summed up by both producers: Two families. One wine. One Passion.

Italian Family Life

Chi si volta, e chi si gira, sempre a casa va finire.

No matter where you go or turn, you
will always end up at home.
- Italian proverb

La famiglia e tutto. Family is everything.
- Italian saying

WHETHER IT'S CONVERSATION with Daniele Rosti or discussions with other predominant Tuscan winemakers here, family and family life always comes out front and center. Before we look at the individuals that are the winemaker stars of this book, let's take a brief look at Italian family life. It, too, shares equal star billing in each of the life stories here.

In Italy, "la famiglia" is sacred. La famiglia means anything and everything related to family. This includes households, homes, houses, communities, and people.

Italiandualcitizenship.net, which helps those learning about Italian family life on the way to becoming official citizens, states that Italian families are loyal and close, extending beyond the immediate family to all the other relatives spanning generations. You will read how individual winemakers here followed their fathers and their families, either to the region or the vocation, as they either moved or stayed in Tuscany.

From the direct and immediate nuclear family to more extended relatives, Italians tend to remain as a close unit spanning generation after generation. Whether they are meeting in a piazza or at someone's home over a large feast, family life in Italy is one of the foundations of Italian culture. Just look around at the Italian families that you know. The emphasis on family and family culture is usually very evident.

Many feel that Italians have stronger feelings of loyalty and sense of family culture than they have to their country. Even if families move away and separate geographically, the family as the center of the social structure, providing harmony, unison, and stability stays completely intact. Beyond this is tremendous emotional support and many times, economical support.

It's not unusual for extended families to live together even after the children are married and have families of their own. In these cases, family continues to be an integral part of everyday life.

There is a deep admiration for elderly family members in Italian culture who are looked up to, usually by the whole family. Senior family members are deeply committed to their children, grandchildren, and other family members, immediate or not. There is always talk about matriarchs and patriarchs in this sense with the older members holding a place of power and respect.

When you think of important Italian family values many aspects come to mind. Spending true quality time, celebrations, religion and religious traditions, and of course, enjoying eating good meals. The women, directed by the grandmother or matriarch, usually prepare and serve the feast, often in the largest home in the family (extended or otherwise) to accommodate everyone. Feasting, over-indulging, and family gatherings all done with great love, enthusiasm, gusto, and joy for life. Seems like this theme gets repeated often when talking about many things Italian.

Italian families stick together through thick and thin.

The family is the foundation of Italian life.

The Italian spirit of family solidarity provides the delight, satisfaction, and enjoyment of life. Don't believe it? Just ask any Italian that you know or encounter. That's why Italian families try to stay bonded and together as long as possible.

Whether it's economic reasons, family reasons, or a desire to preserve nature, Italians return to winemaking traditions and life as winemakers. That was certainly the case for the family of Daniele Rosti. When describing his path to Tuscany and Tuscany winemaking he attributes the return to tradition by his father. You will find similar family ties and stories as the life of each winemaker is featured here.

FATTORIA CASA SOLA

THROW A DART at a dartboard map of Tuscany and chances are you will land on the target area of a Tuscan winery. There are thousands of them with each offering many unique experiences for the senses. Paying a visit to any one of them will delight and bring great joy in your Italian adventures.

One such winery on that fictional dartboard of Tuscany is Fattoria Casa Sola.

So many wineries today are located on the grounds of castles and noble estates and home to long-standing vineyards, as many of these wine production facilities are centuries old. Even if these estates have long since passed from the hands of a noble family, the tradition of wine being made in such places continues into the modern era. One such estate is that of the Fattoria Casa Sola, which is located right smack in the globally famous Tuscan wine-producing region that is the heart of Chianti Classico. Set among vineyards, forestland, and olive groves, the scenery is the evocative and uncontaminated countryside of the past.

Much has already been written about Chianti here. We could write this whole book on the Chianti Classico region alone but have chosen other districts to explore, like Montepulciano, San Gimignano, and other areas processing Sangiovese grapes.

A visit to any locale within Chianti Classico will look much like it did ages ago. Casa Sola is in the town of Barberino in between Florence, Siena, and Pisa in an area often described as quiet, charming, and green.

The winery is situated in an ideal position for visits to all of Tuscany. The beauty of the place and the breathtaking views that can be enjoyed from the farm allow guests to project themselves in full relaxation into the life and culture of the Chianti area.

In the Municipality of Barberino Val d'Elsa, about twenty miles from Florence and a bit further from Siena, Casa Sola covers a total area of 120 hectares of which 30 are planted with vineyards and 40 with olive groves The remaining land is made up of fields and woods which combine to create an enchanting silent and green landscape.

The attention to quality and the rigorous respect for the environment that the vineyard has set for itself require a higher degree of stringency on all cultivation operations first and then in the cellar to ensure those who taste the wines from Casa Sola have an experience that encompasses the emotions of a unique territory.

Not unlike other Tuscan wine producers, this winery strives to obtain the maximum potential from the grapes grown with their passion, experience, expertise, tradition, and innovation. Casa Sola defines their style as "traditional and innovative" in search of the highest quality while respecting their history.

The Gambaro Family has owned and managed Casa Sola for three generations, since 1960, applying their passion and respect for this stunning land into the wine and olive oil produced at this estate.

Under the management of patriarch, Giuseppe Gambaro, Casa Sola had its greatest focus, development, and growth when in 1985 Giuseppe made a commitment to immerse himself personally in the management and direction of the estate. He began to work full time at the winery, utilizing his experience as a manager and his interest and passion for the finer things in life, including Tuscan wine. Giuseppe obtained his knowledge in winemaking by reading as much as he could about notable

Burgundy wines. He secured and advanced his studies with texts and publications about oenology and viticulture, while practicing techniques and methodologies he learned. He began a delicate process and system of vineyard, crop management, machine and equipment renovation, and restoration.

Let's look at his path.

Genoa (Genova) is a port city, the sixth largest city in Italy and the capital of northwest Italy's Liguria region. It's known for its central role in maritime trade over many centuries and still to this day. Genoa has quite a history as it has been one of the most important ports on the Mediterranean: It is currently the busiest port in Italy and in the Mediterranean Sea.

Leaving port life, the water and a maritime environment, Tuscany draws people to it by offering rich culture, stunning landscapes and rolling hills, and traditional, world-class Italian food. Tuscany is the ideal spot to move to, live in and/or visit. These are a few of the reasons native Italians migrate to Tuscany. Tuscany is prototypical Italy.

In the case of Matteo Gambaro, he came with his family after university. Born and schooled in Genoa, the Tuscany aura was like a magnet to him.

Matteo studied at the University of Genoa and decided to pursue agriculture and then viticulture and viniculture. He went on to get an agricultural degree in Florence. (The difference between viniculture and viticulture is viticulture is the science and agriculture of grape growing of all kinds, whether the grape is destined for table grapes or juice grapes. Viniculture is the science and agriculture, also of grapes but only of grapes for winemaking). His educational pursuits included using the local Tuscany vineyard as "his exercise book" for his schooling. He truly was in a valuable position to practice what he was studying.

Casa Sola started as a family business. At the beginning it was more a holiday resort rather than a vineyard. It was owned by Matteo's father and his father's four brothers, along with Matteo's grandfather, Giuseppe Gambaro. As time went on, one of the six family members wanted to invest in the business. Others wanted no part in the investment and wanted the property only for their own holiday. Some did not have any preference, still preferring the sea and sand of Genoa, not the countryside of Tuscany.

Matteo, together with his wife Claudia, had a high desire to share the beauty of the area and land as well as the excellence of high-quality wine, used his real estate knowledge and worked to restore the age-old company homes, giving life to magnificent agriturismos.

For a long time, "agriturismi" (loosely, "Italian vacation farm-holiday homes") have been an Italian accommodation secret that wasn't known or talked about. That has changed. *Travel + Leisure* calls agriturismi Italy's "best affordable spots." An agriturismo with its farm stay environment clearly is the best way to experience Italy and the Tuscan countryside!

Talk about Tuscan winemaking and wineries always incorporates the fact that the best way to experience them is by getting to know the people, visitors, workers, owners, wine experts, and more. There is no better way to achieve this than to actually stay at someone's farm. It's often said, it's not the destination, but the journey. Let me assure you that the destination makes that journey worthwhile. Nothing could be truer when visiting an agriturismo.

The story of the winery is not unlike many other Tuscan winery stories. It was started and greatly influenced by family.

Today, the children of the founder, Matteo and Anna, have moved in to take part in the estate following the family passion. And the story continues....

The growth of Casa Sola is the testimony to the energy, dedication and the commitment of those who work every day at this estate. At Casa Sola, it is the people who work with their enthusiasm, their passion, and their experience and expertise which have allowed all of Casa Sola to reach high levels of production and quality of wines and olive oil.

Around Tuscany, the world`s best olive oils are made with the same care and passion as the fine wines of the region. The life of an olive tree is longer than that of a winemaker's life; the trees exist for hundreds of years. Olive trees have been planted in and around Italian and Tuscan vineyards for thousands of years.

Many of the methods used today in making olive oil are very similar to those in pre-Roman times. Since discussions of just about every Tuscan winery, especially Casa Sola, involve talk about olive and olive oil production, it's worth taking a deeper look at it.

Olive oil is an important product for Casa Sola. Since the beginning, this winery has always dedicated great attention and care to the olive trees on their land. High quality olive oil must be made from healthy fruit. Because of this, the care and harvesting is done free of any need for chemical fertilizers or pesticides.

At Casa Sola, the olive groves and the vineyards are staggered one from the other: The different crop rotation is a simple and effective way to create natural barriers against the diffusion of parasites and other environmental influences.

Planting olive trees in and around vineyards serves wine producers in two ways. Primarily, that is to produce two profitable crops efficiently without substantially increasing the amount of land used and keeping resources used at a minimum.

Olives and grapes make great companion plants because they like the same climate. Olives and grapes are self-pollinating, not relying on pollen carriers to jump from flower to flower. Looking at some grape/olive fields you will see grape vines sheltered by olive trees, protecting them from wild weather, gusty winds, and other environmental influences that could disrupt co-existence and/or pollination.

The road to Vinci, home of Leonardo da Vinci is filled with olive groves. Leonardo`s birthplace was and continues to be full of olive groves. Leonardo is famous for many things; one little known fact about him is that among his inventions were variations of two olive presses.

Just when summer ends and winemakers look forward to quieter, less active times, olive harvesting season approaches. Olives are picked from the trees, sometimes half ripe, taken to the milling area right after, and pressed. What results is that extra virgin olive oil that all Italians and many non-Italians delight in—the dipping of warm, fresh bread into freshly milled olive oil. There is nothing like doing it at the time of processing, in Italy, on the spot in the olive mill/winery. Often the fruits of the labors, olive oil and wine, exist on the same table during mealtime.

Olive groves continue to mature as the late grape harvests conclude. This is usually around the November time frame. This harvest continues until frost takes over, thus ending the olive growing/harvesting season. The harvest seasons of each crop, the grapes and the olives, are truly complementary to one another.

We can discuss the landscape, the soils and even the grapes but the heartbeat of the farm and winery is the wine cellar. As Matteo states, it is here that passion, experience, tradition, and innovation blend together to reach the highest expression of the Casa Sola grapes.

Matteo explains that the Casa Sola wine cellar undergoes continuous innovation in order to guarantee an increasing quality-oriented production.

It is within the wine cellar that the winemaker spends a lot of his time during his workday. The time spent consists of various duties, almost like balancing spinning plates on many spindles.

Are all winemakers' days the same? They are and they aren't. When you ask any Tuscan winemaker what a typical day consists of you will invariably get two answers. One is that no day is like another; every day is different in terms of opportunities, challenges, and progress. The other answer is all the activity that starts to sound similar from winemaker to winemaker usually centers around outdoor crop production and management to inside the cellar wine-making operations.

Matteo Gambarro is no different. He starts off describing his daily activities where he is lucky enough to work with nature and the outdoors. His work is very much influenced by the wine growing and production season. He, like many entrepreneurs and successful, driven principals, wishes he could be more proactive and progressive but sometimes nature doesn't allow it.

Dealing with nature is the romantic part of the job. Dealing with cold winters and hot summers, not so romantic. In the summer, grapes are growing and maturing. There is a lot of outdoor activity. Matteo is outside tending to crop management early in the morning to avoid the hottest of temperatures. Outside he is checking vegetation, vine growing, the stress of the elements and the natural evolution of grapes. He truly monitors growing and maturation of the grapes. Once it gets hot, he migrates back inside to his office or to the cellar.

In the winter there is an opposite approach; it is mostly office work and only on "mild" winter days does he venture outside for outdoor activity. It goes without saying that in the winter cellar activities are on the increase and in the forefront; the cellar is much more active. Activity centers around analyzing the previous harvest—the grapes and eventual wine char-

Al Lautenslager

acteristics—and deciding where each product goes (type of wine, variety, brand, bottle). These elemental stresses that Matteo speaks of are primarily climatic in nature and result in monitoring and shifting of agricultural production patterns. These, in turn, impact the overall ecosystem and economic and cultural perspectives of the wines produced.

Every day, the winemaker must check environmental threats. These could be sunlight-related, the temperature, water, soil influences (terroir), and normal vegetation processes of the vines. Yields and quality are a function of the successful management of these stresses. Monitoring these daily allows the winemaker to develop the proper response strategies to deal with these elemental stresses.

That's the busy day and daily activity of the successful winemaker and as you can see it's not all tasting, romance, and celebration...yet.

In speaking of this winemaker's success, Matteo's and Casa Sola's best success is when true winemaking and the balance of activities is fulfilled and when he sees himself and the winery progressing in all aspects of wine production.

His role is considered by many to be romantic, but there are hard times. One key factor contributing to his success is discipline. His philosophy of discipline is one of three parts that drives him and his business, eventually equaling success. Those parts are satisfaction, discipline, and passion. The passion component is always present when talking to Tuscan winemakers, but Matteo extends that with his satisfaction goal and the discipline factor in the work.

There is an old saying, be careful of what you ask for; you might get it. That certainly is the case here, with Matteo Gambarro. Whether he states it or not that is what he was seeking when following his family into the winemaking vocation. His start was similar to others but also different in many ways.

Owners of Casa Sola for three generations, the Gambarro family has managed the company since 1960. It was in 1985 Giuseppe Gambarro decided to immerse himself in the management of the estate and began to work full time at the company. He had considerable management experience to contribute, as well as a sense of curiosity and passion for the finer things in life. You can count Tuscan wine in this category.

Matteo's parents retired from this winemaking estate, leaving him to be the primary viticulturist. His sister is involved managing the accommodations for visitors to the estate along with his wife, who is partly involved. His dream is that the next generation will take over from him but that is still far away as his daughter is only 12 years old. His vision is that she will develop the same passions and have a possible role very soon but she is, of course, still a long way from fuller responsibilities related to the winery.

Just like many Tuscan winemaker's paths, you can see a great influence from family life. Studying with and under his father, along with his formal studies, helped Matteo to further develop philosophies for his winemaking, whether personal or professional.

Just like his father and much like his fellow winemakers, there is, within his job, spirit, attitude and vision, a great respect for nature and the environment that they work and live in. The Gambarro family always believed, and it carries on to today, that there is great passion and vision to think about and care for the next generation, leaving the world a better place than he found it for those that follow him. That passion pervades throughout Casa Sola. It sounds very philosophical, but Matteo brings it back into practice by stating it is more a goal. He feels strongly that what they put into bottles is just not the next wine but is the beauty, history, culture, and tradition of winemaking and his family.

Those at Casa Sola under the leadership and ownership of Matteo Gambarro strive to make wine like the winery has for the past 100 years. With that though, they like to continue to evolve and add things that reflect their own personal touches. While they are not big fans of the latest and greatest technology, they are interested in always improving, saving time which according to Matteo results in making ordinary wine in an extraordinary way. He emphasizes there is nothing new nor fancy; just proper time management and accomplishing the essential parts of good winemaking.

This does, however, fly in the face of making wine and winemaking heritage part of the community, almost more global in nature. The whole community of winemakers is "as strong as a forest, with strong diversity from each winery owner." This further implies different components of Italian culture.

In any talk of anything Italian, culture always is mentioned. It is written about here.

We all think we understand culture and live with our own cultures. To expound on the whole concept of culture, just take a look at the Wikipedia definition and description:

Culture is an umbrella term which encompasses the social behavior and norms found in human societies, as well as the knowledge, beliefs, arts, customs, capabilities, and habits of the individuals in these groups.

The components of this definition as stated could be the subjects and topics of its own book. In this case we will look at the culture of Italian winemakers and the lives they live.

Matteo of Casa Sola loves to talk about his culture. He states that tradition and innovation are key parts to his culture and those that work with him at Casa Sola. Part of tradition is learning what was done in the past and not making the same mistakes going forward. He extends his cultural discussion by talking about maintaining the spirit of the land and what it offers to you in life and winemaking.

Tradition is made up of many parts: history, nature, and more. The whole Chianti region is rich in all of this. You will find many, including Matteo, that culturally want to make a good product where its origin is the beauty of the land. This carries through to his dream of having consumers of the Casa Sola wines have a strong feeling of Tuscany, whether it be sensory or intellectual, when drinking their wines.

The more you talk about Italian culture, the more you realize that Italian culture is steeped in the arts, family, architecture, music, and food. Home of the Roman Empire, the many Tuscan landscapes and a major center of the Renaissance, culture on the Italian peninsula has flourished for centuries. Italian lifestyle and culture are largely imitated all over the world. It is made up of small and big habits that create a peculiar and sought-after image. Italians value and celebrate all aspects of life. Spending time with family and friends, eating and drinking well, and enjoying beauty in all its forms ranks right at the top of life's priorities for Italians.

Let's just say that the Italian culture is known for enjoying the finer things in life.

In viewing an online video of the Casa Sola story, Matteo talks about the "secret" of Casa Sola. He breaks down all that we have reviewed here very simply.

He starts by mentioning the enchanting view of this area of the Chianti Classico region. He mixes beauty, the location, and the passion to make something ordinary in an extraordinary way. It's that simple.

He talks about incorporating the history, the traditions, and the land/terroir into their wine production.

He furthers this simplification by talking about the constant monitoring during the fermentation process and applying a caring nature during the "wine rest." He concludes this secret with the sound of quietness, "Shhhhhhh."

Casa Sola has experts that taste and re-taste, searching for the best of the best from the process. They couple this with the respectfulness of the environment and a culture of excellence to produce a wine product that is, "unique, special and of high quality," concluding with the thoughtful, personal, and reflective statement of providing "unforgettable Tuscan flavors." That's the Casa Sola way, the Casa Sola secret, the culture and tradition of this Tuscan delight.

Matteo is proud to make a very profound

statement of his vision and dreams. He will tell you that one of these is to get every person who visits Tuscany and/or his winery to have a liquid memory of a lifetime. Many leave, go home, and return over and over to relive those memories and to create more along a sensory journey of wine tasting and wine drinking. For wine, it's the start of the Tuscan life and the Tuscan journey.

As we leave Casa Sola, Matteo offers some words of wisdom. He says to keep following the luxury of simplicity. Value what you have around you and always try to add value to what you have. It's time to expand your thinking and Italian winemaking thinking. The next move here is to think globally. Yes, there are still lots of local influences: Matteo uses the term Glocal—thinking globally while remaining local. Finally, he says to value the diversity, whether it's the soils, the grapes, or the variety of wines coming from the Tuscan region.

TENUTA VALDIPIATTA

"It's allowed to drink without being thirsty."

I CAN SHARE WITH you the passion of Tuscany winemakers, the typical workdays, the land and surroundings, and the family influences, and I will, but nothing characterizes the spirit of Tuscany wine more than a famous wine quotation predominantly displayed at the Tenuta Valdipiatta.

Emblazoned on a sturdy, colorful plaque, hung in an aging cellar is the famous quote, in Latin: "Licet sitis sine siti." At first glance it looks medieval, foreign, and famous. Upon further digging and interpretation, the quote, perfect for this winery and other Tuscan winemaking sites, translates to "It's allowed to drink without being thirsty." The owners take great pride in this and say it is their motto, on full display to welcome all of their guests.

The quote is from *Carmina Burana*, a manuscript of many poems, dramatic texts, and bawdy songs, mostly from the 11th and 12th century that reflect an international crusade based in Europe.

In Italy—whether at home or at a restaurant—where there is food, there is wine. Wine is meant to heighten and enrich the taste of the food and it's considered an essential part of a meal—not a fancy treat. It's repeated here but it's very common with anything Tuscany oriented. Nothing here suggests thirst more, the Tenuta Valdipiatta motto completely intact.

Italians drink wine all day—it doesn't really matter what time it is or better yet, the drinking of Italian wine can happen at any time of day. That is certainly the notion behind "Licet sitis sine siti."

Wine is more than just something to drink for Italians. Wines of all types are a very important part of their culture, originating in ancient times. It's rare to find any Italian person who doesn't like wine or doesn't drink it, or any meal served without it. The prominence and distinction of Italian wine dates back to ancient times and Pliny the Elder, who is sometimes considered the first wine critic and the author of the work titled *Naturalis Historia* (Natural History).

From this comes the famous saying"in vino, veritas" or in English—in wine, there is truth.

This truth turns into the fact that it's always wine o'clock for natives and usually for visitors, too. It's allowed and you don't have to be thirsty to visit wine o'clock.

I share all this with you to give you the flavor (pun intended) of life at Tenuta Valdipiatta.

Throughout we have learned and are learning about the character of Tuscany. Now that we have this characterization where we can drink wine without being thirsty, let's look at the "flavor" and characterization of the vineyard. The flavor of a vineyard is truly a function of the owner. Of course, the land, climate, process, and end product are part of that flavor and characterization but without a passionate owner, it's just another winery.

Founder, Giulio Caporali handed the running of Valdipiatta over to his daughter Miriam in 2002. Miriam was well prepared, having studied business in Rome and winemaking in Bordeaux. Miriam stated that, "What I learned there was that smooth-tasting wines with unique and interesting flavors could only be made with environmentally respectful grape-growing and sensitive winemaking."

Today Miriam is not only the owner but the general manager in charge of sales and public relations. As a young entrepreneur and a Business Administrator graduate from the University of Rome, Miriam decided to dedicate herself to the family business after extensive experience in consulting. From 1997 to 2002, Miriam worked closely at her father's side at Valdipiatta, learning all the various aspects of winery management. She also visited Bordeaux, where she took advanced classes in wine tasting and winemaking. Sharing her father's passion for Montepulciano's terroir and its ancient winemaking tradition, she decided to dedicate herself completely to the family business.

Tradition to her is as important as the passion for the entire winemaking process. She states that she is firmly connected with her family's tradition, which makes for superior wines at a superior Tuscan winery. While this tradition is tried and true, she is careful that it does not prevent tunnel vision and a narrow viewpoint of things. She still wants to keep what came from the past, simple things like the barrels for winemaking and storage. She states that it is something that feels proper for her wines and for Vino Nobile.

Miriam arrived in Tuscany much like many other winery owners. She arrived in Tuscany following the desires and passions of her father. Guilio realized his dream of becoming a winemaker at the young age of 50. He left a career as an engineer working in a big city to becoming a passionate grower of the Sangiovese grape, other Tuscan grapes, and winemaking. His choice to fulfill this passion of making his own wine in one of the more beautiful preserved, rural environments in the world (beautiful by those who live in and those who have visited), Montepulciano. He simply wanted to create a great wine.

Valdipiatta has always been family-owned. It was founded in the 1960s by the original owner and acquired at the end of the 1980s by Giulio Caporali. It wasn't until his purchase that the winery began to earn a reputation for producing some of the finest Vino Nobile di Montepulciano. Through his vision, determination, hard work, and passion he transformed this small Tuscan farmhouse and its vineyard into a modern-day successful vineyard. He studied soils, vine cloning, pruning systems, and the like. His vision included replanting to produce Sangiovese grapes of superior quality. Giulio followed these same methods and standards as he purchased additional vineyards in the fruitful grape growing areas of Montepulciano. His passion, methods, and vision carried through to updated wine cellar operations, storage, and distribution.

Since we are emphasizing family and its importance in Italy and the pursuit of passions from one generation to the next like the Caporalis at Valdipiatta, it's worth noting the patriarch and winery founder, Giulio was a great student of the history of Vino Nobile and the town of Montepulciano. He has translated a 700-year-old text of medieval law regulating the production and trade of local wine. He has also written about Porsenna, the legendary founder of the town and the last king of Rome, an Etruscan king known for his war against the city of Rome. An eager scholar, Giulio translated from Latin the charter of the town of Montepulciano, a manuscript from the 14th century and wrote and published an essay on the Etruscan origins of the name of Montepulciano.

With a unique and focused approach and respect for the land (terroir), Giulio advanced Valdipiatta to be one of the top producers of the Vino Nobile di Montepulciano grapes and wines. "It is my Shangri-La" is how Giulio described Valdipiatta. This belief and the legacy of Giulio continues through his daughter's ownership of Valdipiatta.

Miriam's dream is a continuance of her late father's: to enhance the whole of their land. Valdipiatta is an estate vineyard and winery located in southeastern Tuscany, between Rome and Florence, in the very heart of the Vino Nobile di Montepulciano district. The estate comprises 100 acres of land, at an average of 1,200 feet above sea level.

Montepulciano has over 2,500 years of wine-growing history. Its red wines are made from Italy's signature red wine grape, the Sangiovese or Prugnolo as locals call it. According to grapecollective.com, "Vino Nobile" is an historic term most commentators ascribe to the 16th century when the pope's cellar master praised the wines from the Tuscan town of Montepulciano as being fit for "noblemen" and the name stuck. In this case the wine is a rich red from mainly Sangiovese grapes. It is one of the three major Sangiovese-producing regions in Tuscany alongside Montalcino and Chianti. Here, as with Chianti, the mixture of other grape varieties is permitted, and Sangiovese must comprise at least 70% of the wine.

There are other interpretations as to where "Vino Nobile" came from, according to Miriam. She states that the one that is the most trustworthy is the fact that in Montepulciano, the Nobile family were living in the town. In the town there is currently the Nobile Building. Their land, their vineyards were all around the hill of Montepulciano, a very close-knit town, not spread out like the countryside of the Chianti area. Due to this, the owners of the wineries were able to personally work in the winery, and institute an owner's check of the quality of the wine as if it was from the eyes, viewpoint, and approval of the Nobile family. This only elevated the quality and ensuing reputation of the wines produced.

Consumers and drinkers of the Vino Nobile di Montepulciano can expect a fruity wine. Of course, in wine tasting, fruity is a relative term. The fruit and grape of Sangiovese is a red fruity taste with hints of blackberries. Winemakers and aficionados say there is a complexity that comes from the related vineyards. This leads to an often-used term to describe these wines as being elegant. Miriam states that the Vino Nobile is not necessarily a powerful wine; it's a wine that can be identified by its finesse. This is one superior quality that identifies the Vino Nobile in general. This flavor and this description characterizes this winery, characterizes the Tuscan land, and the heart of Montepulciano as well as the family, the people, and multi-generational ownership.

Miriam Caporali's daily activity is different from day to day. This is the case of every winemaker interviewed. In fact, Miriam will state that there is not a "typical day."

In a nutshell, Miriam Caporali's job and daily life as a winemaker is basically her walking the vineyards observing grapes growing on vines planted in sandy soils, dense clay, and other terroir variations. She then follows and watches closely the picking and the fermenting process all the way to bottling. Obviously, she manages and follows several activities depending, as she says, on the moment of the year; not the moment of the day or a moment in time; it's the moment of the year. This addresses the seasonality of activities within the winemaking process as well as other related activities.

As an example, in the hot summer months, especially in August, her day starts early at 6:30 am. The first activity of the day is checking on, taking care of, and monitoring bees and earthworms that are used for humus production.

Before talking about bees and earthworms, let's look at a quick word on humus as Miriam talks about it:

Humus (not to be confused with hummus, the spread or dip commonly eaten in the Middle East) is partially decomposed organic matter made up of decayed plant or animal matter. Humus provides nutrients for plants and increases the ability of soil to retain water.

Due to the limited presence of water and nutrients in grapevine bearing soils, the grapes go to the ripening phase earlier. As a result, the aromas and bouquets mature faster, the grapes get higher sugar levels and the amount of acids drops earlier, all essential in quality winemaking with all having to be managed, almost daily by the winemaker.

Grapes are grown in deep, fertile soil where they produce a surprising amount of robustness (and fruit!). Vineyards are planted in soils based on a mix of sand, clay, silt, chalk, and limestone.

For all soil types—either the rich clay soils or the poor sandy soils—humus is the most important source of nitrogen and phosphate compounds. Higher nitrogen levels result in more vegetative growth of the grapevine, and grapes with less concentrated aromas. Humus provides a reservoir for the plant nutrients available in the soil for balanced plant growth.

Humus can be produced naturally or through a process called composting. When people compost, they collect decaying organic material, such as plants and animals, that are then turned into soil.

This includes the function, dead or alive, of bees and earthworms in winemaking.

At first glance you might ask why bees and earthworms are important in the production of grapes for winemaking and why someone like Miriam watches over and tends to them. Bees are essential in vineyards and winemaking and actually do have a vital, principal role in wine production.

Maintaining the soil for the optimum grape production depends on many components of the eco-system. One of these contributing to the agricultural health is the nitrogen balance. Grapevines can self-fertilize (are wind-pollinated), however bees are the main pollinators for other plants and vegetation that benefit a good nitrogen balance in vineyard soils and contribute to a healthy vine environment. This along with other soil/water balance mechanisms supports the natural replenishment of other important soil nutrients, essential for the ideal crop production and an increase in the organic content of soils.

Having a sustainable ecosystem and biodiversity is the key for any organic winegrower that wants to maintain a thriving ecosystem; that's why several of them have their own beehives near vineyards.

According to Fred Loimer, ranked amongst the best wine producers in Austria, "Earthworms can also be a great tool for a winemaker. They are great indicators of soil health and incredibly useful, because they create precious humus by helping to degrade plant matter. They also make it easier for rainwater to enter and be retained in the soil, and slowing water uptake by the vines, creating a healthier vine and grape supply."

Valdipiatta's Sangiovese vines grow on these soils, rich in sand, with the sustaining ecosystems as described here. The resulting wines are richly fruited but not heavy or overbearing or, as described by the winemakers, tough. The adoption of these organic, eco-friendly, wine-growing practices by Miriam Caporali has given the wines, according to Miriam, added brightness. Bright is a term used for vivid, focused, and flavorful young wines. Bright wines are fresh, ripe, zesty, and lively. This is a descriptive term, basically, used in reference to the character of wine. The term bright is also used to describe the appearance of wine in a glass.

When asked about the education of a superior winemaker, Miriam expounds about her French winemaking training and time in Bordeaux, France. Miriam's decision to study in and learn from the best winemakers in Bordeaux about how to pick the grapes at the perfect moment for maximum smoothness has given Valdipiatta's Vino Nobile wines intriguing texture and character of superiority. Those who argue that Vino Nobile is among Tuscany's most exciting regions surely look to estates like Valdipiatta as one winery that makes that excitement a reality.

Now back to the winemaker's daily activity.

After the first of task of checking earthworm and bee activity, and giving attention to the organic eco-systems, Miriam usually meets the agronomist on staff at Valdipiatta. Daily activity is reviewed, and an update is reviewed regarding the activity in the vineyard and the eventual planning for anything related to cellar operations. This includes moving harvested grapes from the vineyard, crushing, aging, blending laboratories, bottling and packaging all the way to finished goods inventory and consumer experiences and distribution.

Miriam described further daily activity to grapecollective.com as follows: "It is very important to know your vineyards, to know the behavior and the history of the winery. First, you have to taste the grapes. Then we make a chemical analysis of the grapes. We not only do a sugar and acidity analysis, but we also analyze about 12 to 13 other different parameters. Once we have the result of the tasting, mixed, crossed together with the chemical analysis, we are much more knowledgeable about the raw material that we have in the vineyard, and we are more able to conduct the vinification, and get the result that we really want for the wine. You're basically using scientific methods to make sure you have the capacity to make a wine that's nice and smooth."

With all this talk about biodiversity and eco-systems it's important to look at the soils, the terroir in Montepulciano.

The terroir in Montepulciano, is quite homogeneous. All the vineyards in Montepulciano are very concentrated around the hill of Montepulciano. The composition of the soil is a mix of tufa (a porous rock composed of calcium carbonate and formed by precipitation from water) and very old sand and clay. At Valdipiatta in particular, there is mostly sandy soil vineyards in the deepest part, around 300 meters above sea level and soil with a very high clay content on the top, yet still underground.

Miriam states that the secret of the "elegance" of the wines in Montepulciano is that the combination of the sand and clay allows the water to be drained through the sand, which is usually on top. At the same time, the clay keeps the water and the ground moist like a sponge. It sounds inconsistent and almost humorous but an old vineyard that is 50 years old can still find the water in the ground. Remaining water in the ground helps to keep the freshness and the acidity for future grapes. These things are paid great attention to as the owner manages the land for current and future grape production as well as planning harvests and related activity.

Aside from crop management and winemaking there is lots of activity spent in the latter stages of getting wine to the consumer: consumer sales, consumer wine tastings, winery visits, welcoming of private guests, winery tours, and related support activity.

In summary, it is an important activity in the day of a winemaker to tour the vineyard to check the sanitary status of the vines and the ripening process. This is all happening during the summertime, a very seasonal part of the job, when there is less travel by Miriam for promotions, following Italian and foreign markets, and related marketing activities.

Understanding a Tuscan winemaker and

their life wouldn't be complete without a visit to some personal philosophies.

Miriam proudly states that one of her favorite personal philosophies is, "Do what you love and love what you do." It is worth understanding her perspective here. Simply stated, this means that she loves the work of doing what she does every day. The love of doing what you love leads to happiness, satisfaction, fulfillment, and success. Confucius's take on this is "Choose a job you love, and you will never have to work a day in your life."

A lot of people say, "Pursue your dreams/passions." Successful, happy, and fulfilled people fall in love with what they're doing, which is much more important. Miriam's view on life and work reflects this.

Miriam talks at length about being very lucky to have the opportunity to follow her father in what she considers one of the most beautiful jobs a person can have. She truly does consider working with wine, with nature and natural surroundings a gift. Miriam is a glass half full type of person in all the activities of her job, good or bad. Yes, there are unpleasantries as there are with any job and dealing with the Italian bureaucracy is one of those. She still finds a way to see that glass half full.

Taking philosophies even further, she states that her deepest philosophy aside from doing what you love is to respect the health of the soil, the biodiversity of the ecosystem around her, and the authenticity of her terroir. She takes responsibility to take good care of the land where she grows her vineyards thinking that beside and around the vineyards there is a flora and fauna that has to be integrated and not depleted by her winemaking activities.

Winemakers like Miriam like to talk about what's next. She will tell anyone willing to listen that the next stage is making more and more consumers aficionados and people who understand Vino Nobile as not only a superior wine but as an experience to remember. This is done when you experience the environment and when you know the culture of where the wine evolved. Touring and visiting is essential. Communication about the wines, the culture, and the appreciation has to happen. It requires coming together in the production of Vino Nobile. Miriam talks about the consortium that helps with this. Producers need to be united, all in one direction and not go astray in too many different directions. That only confuses the marketplace and consumers, and this wine has too much at stake to make that happen.

According to grapecollective.com, wines in this territory have been made for over a thousand years. The tradition of making wine is in the blood of the winemakers and the families.

The lands in Montepulciano have always been producing good grapes. Vino Nobile has been known for hundreds of years and still today, the producers pay careful attention to the complexity, and the culture that the wine came from. Attention to detail is so high that people can perceive this by drinking the wine itself. A glass of Vino Nobile wine encompasses the terroir of Montepulciano, the culture, the history, the gastronomy, and everything else.

So there you have philosophies, work activity, information on the region, and perspectives on everything involved in winemaking that truly make this one winemaker superior in all of Tuscany. Let's look at others.

.

LA MATTERAIA

A FEW KILOMETERS FROM Florence, north of Tuscany, among the rolling highlands, soaring landscapes, and against the background of mountain peaks, summits, and gaps of passage, spans the territory of the Mugello. Here you find both babbling brooks and silent waters, an engaging countryside populated with friendly, peaceful, social townsfolk and people working with energy and commitment, robust Italian food, historical places of the Medici, and other historical sites and villas. Wow. That's a lot of Tuscan flavors that make you want to be there right this instant.

The Romagna Apennines region in northern Italy is known for its medieval cities and countryside, rich Italian food and fare, and some of the finest Italian seaside resorts. The capital,

Bologna, is an energetic city with an 11th-century architecture lining the streets and piazzas of its old-world core. Ravenna, near the Adriatic coast, is known and visited for its brightly colored Byzantine mosaics. The Mugello valley region between the Sieve River and the foot of the Apennines that mark the border between Tuscany and Emilia-Romagna, Italy is considered to be the heart of the Italian Alps.

Set in this valley and buried in the Tuscan countryside is the village of Vicchio. Here you can take in breathtaking views, amidst olive and vine covered areas at the base of the Apennine Mountains, truly, a peaceful and natural setting. It was considered the "new frontier" of the Florentine Republic region when it was established in the Middle Ages. In 1324, the Florentine Republic fortified the village. Since that moment the village, Vicchio, has experienced a period of economic growth.

A visit to the village of Vicchio takes you to The La Matteraia farm. The farm and wine growing estate are at the foot of the Tuscan-Romagna Apennines.

La Matteraia is a family-owned and operated vineyard, winery, and guesthouse that produces exclusive wines of northern Italian origin and offers guests stunning views of the Mugello Valley, vineyard, and olive tree groves along with intimate wine and olive oil tastings in a pleasant and comfortable environment. It is billed as the place to visit if you want to embrace the charm of a Tuscan family wine business.

The story of La Matteraia is a familiar one of Tuscany wine producers: family, tradition, passion, nature, top-quality wines. This is a recurring theme. That theme is no different for Ivan Mirko, son of the founder, Ivo Malpaga.

Ivan continues the story of passion. He talks of growing up in his grandfather's cellar where, as a child, he literally wandered among full vats of wine; a memory held by many of the children in the mountains of Trento. Ivan and his family had a strong desire to continue the intense Trentino history and raise his family in the Tuscan hills, where in the early 70s Ivan's father purchased the farm, land, and potential for passionate winemaking.

Ivan's grandfather's native Trento is famous for the beauty of its landscape and the quality of its snow, making it a favorite destination for ski enthusiasts. These northernmost areas of Italy are close to the Austrian border. The jagged peaks of the Dolomite Mountain range stretch skyward, creating a notable backdrop to one of the world's most important wine-producing areas: Trentino. This region of Ivan's grandfather formed the basis of the passion the family wanted to transplant to Tuscany. From a winemaking standpoint, Trentino, is considered Northern Italy's Wine Mecca. The path was then natural to go from Trentino in the north to the southern winemaking region of Tuscany.

Some of the notable characteristics of the area are the peaks and hilltops of the region that protect the lands from the elements, casting a rain shadow over the valley. The slopes and hillsides channel warm air, heating and cooling the land over the course of the day. This mountain breeze and winds, in turn, keeps vineyards free from undesirable microbe activity and fungal diseases, almost the perfect climatic conditions for vineyard farming and wine development.

Viticulture meteorological note (wine-searcher.com): "Rain shadow is a geo-meteorological phenomenon of great importance to viticulture. The rain shadow area is one of elevated topography that blocks the passage of rainclouds between two points. The effect creates a "shadow" on the downwind side, where precipitation is much lower than on the upwind side. This provides, in this region's case, a true benefit for viticulture."

These conditions explain why Trentino has the notable winemaking heritage that Ivan experienced and learned from and what has earned it its Mecca status described earlier.

It is this heritage, passion, and legacy that the Malpaga family wanted to transplant into the Tuscany Region.

Ivan says it best when he states that when he took over the operation of the winery that he wanted to weave his history, his family's history, and his own memories to bring about the fulfillment of his dream of opening, owning, and managing a winery, as his grandfather did. He, much like most Italians, was aware of the important past behind him but also was sure of his vision and expectations going forward. Those are all the driving forces behind Italian tradition and the individual winemaking legacies of the many families involved.

Continuing along the family, tradition, passion theme, Ivan states that he has a great passion for wine and much curiosity and interest in everything that surrounds it. Leonardo Da Vinci had a great passion and drive for curiosity. Many parallels from his line of thinking can be drawn to compare with the forward-thinking approaches of many Tuscan winemakers, especially in the case of La Matteraia and Ivan Mirko.

Normally going to the dictionary to understand a Da Vinci concept is not the first thing to do but when it comes to the concept of curiosity it's like Da Vinci authored the definition (*Da-Vinci Visits Today*). Simply put, that definition is a strong desire to know or learn something. That's Leonardo's whole life captured in one sentence, essentially. Of course, there is more, but when thinking about his desire for learning, that's what drove him to his pinnacle.

Curiosity is a common characteristic of geniuses, now, in the past and will be in the future, whether you are the chief Renaissance man of Italian history or today's Tuscan winemaker in central Italy.

Leonardo da Vinci kept a zealous and fanatical curiosity throughout life, including at the prime of his career. Yes, that almost is the definition of being insatiable.

He once said, "The noblest pleasure is the joy of understanding."

As I discuss in my book, *Da Vinci Visits Today*, Leonardo's observation and belief that "everything connects" was the basis of much of his work. Making connections between some of the simplest and seemingly unrelated things is one of the most crucial creative and critical thinking skills anyone can ever master.

It bears repeating that Da Vinci, without question, had a very curious mind. He quickly realized that a curious mind could relate, process, and connect ideas quicker and better. Leonardo's genius qualities and talents were not a result of built-in mental brilliance. They were a product of all of this curiosity and the common themes discussed and actions he took on his findings. Many people ask questions and get answers, but not many take action on what they learn. All of those outcomes and satisfactions would be recorded in his notebooks along with a list of more questions, a pathway of action, and more answers. His notebooks were a curiosity "gold mine."

He chose to live boldly and differently from others during his time. He was never one to settle, especially as it related to learning and satisfying curiosity after curiosity.

Regardless of what he called it, Da Vinci woke up every day, much like today's Tuscan winemakers, thinking about pursuing what interested him most and knew that by following his interests and pursuits he would accomplish his goal of continuously learning.

Italian master Leonardo Da Vinci is the poster child of curiosity. There is no doubt that same level of curiosity is ingrained in Ivan's mindset and thinking and in his approach to Tuscan winemaking.

Aside from the cerebral approach to Tuscan winemaking, Ivan works according to his dream and economic possibility and the goal of being a respected winemaker with his own working processes.

He is hard working with great attention to detail with his mission constantly in front of him.

When looking at typical workdays at the Tuscan wineries, every person in charge will tell you that no day is like any other day; they differ depending on many factors. Ivan at La

Matteraia approaches the description of his workday a little differently. He has classified his days to fit into one of three types.

He can just about tell you that any day he is at work at the winery it will be patterned after one of three typical days.

Ivan's first typical day is one regarding the period at the beginning of the year where most of a day's work activity centers around the care of the crops. Care of the crops, in this case involves pruning of the vines, applying vine and plant treatments, vine training, and more.

Vine training is the process of directing and controlling growth of the vine to form a vine with the desired shape and structure. The main goal of training the vine in the development year is to create a well-established root system. The winemaker focuses on establishing a strong and vigorous root system that builds storage for nutrients to enhance growth in subsequent years of winemaking.

The desired outcome is a vine with specific dimensions. Proper vine training is essential for producing a good yield of high-quality fruit and maintaining a balance between vegetative vine growth and harvested fruiting. Training and yearly pruning of grapevines is crucial, otherwise the winery will end up with an overgrown entangled mess which affects the quality and yield of a particular harvest.

There are dozens, if not hundreds of different methods of training grapes and providing vine care, depending on the grape variety, the geographical areas, and the desired wine resulting from the different grape varieties. Vine care and the focus of this type of typical day also includes the menial activities of vine watering, weed control, pest control, and fertilizer application.

The vine balance component of vine care is providing a state at which vegetative and reproductive growth can be sustained indefinitely while maintaining healthy growth, adequate fruit production, and desired fruit quality (sugar levels, acid balance, and flavor compounds).

The second type of typical day is one that is dedicated to welcoming customers, visitors at the winery for wine tastings in the wine cellar, and shoppers, whether they be tourists or natives from the area restocking their own personal wine supply.

Any winery that wants their product to be purchased, appreciated, tasted, consumed, and done so with a repeat cycle needs to pay attention to interaction with customers. This includes visits to the winery by tourists or other groups and associated wine tastings. This activity doesn't happen by itself and needs attention from the winemaker/owner and ambassador of the winery. In the Tuscan land, wine tours are popular and in demand from people all over the world.

For the successful Tuscan wineries, there are many benefits to including tours and tastings as an integral part of their marketing strategy. Anytime a visitor visits the winery they can see behind-the-scenes activity that normally is not experienced or witnessed by the non-touring, drinking public. Dinners and themed events in the vineyard set them apart from other wineries in the area.

This is the start or continuance of a relationship between winery and customer/consumer. Relationships lead to experiences and experiences lead to referrals, endorsements, and repeat purchases.

Ivan knows that attention spent on the activities of this typical day pay off. He knows he has a group of engaged and enthusiastic people who want to know more about the wines they drink, the Tuscan region, and the brand and identity of the winery they are visiting. Ivan takes great pride in the fact that two of his children, now in their early to mid-twenties are involved in the business. They concentrate on reception, the sale of products and social media marketing that continues to raise the profile of the product and the winery. Ivan and other employees classify all of this marketing/sales activity as paying attention to the "careful" sale of the wine. Of course, he includes the general approach of marketing in anything related to sales. The pay-off is that the company and products are better known in the area thus justifying the appropriate amount of time to marketing.

As has been said, behind every successful man is a successful and supporting woman. Ivan's wife, Sabrina, a native of the town of Vicchio, plays a fundamental role in the support and offering of ideas, comments, and opinions for all the company projects and strategic direction. She works with the same passion as her husband and adds a whole other level of support to the vineyard and operation.

The third typical day consists of work dedicated exclusively to activities in the cellar (winemaking, decanting, filtering, bottling and labeling).

In the cellar it usually seems as if the work is endless. After the first phases of winemaking, the decanting and filtering, there is always bottling and labeling.

The second phase of winemaking discussed here includes pressing, cleaning, fermenting, drying, crushing, destemming, raking, alcohol fermentation and all of the associated maintenance to the process components throughout.

The aim of all of these second phase activities is to extract all the best components from the skins while keeping important components active and well oxygenated.

The planned wines, after blending based on type, varietal, affinity, and other complementary features, are put in tanks for storage which is then completed once the acid is transformed which adds body to the wine and balances the desired acidity. From here, off the wine goes to a segregated part of the cellar for storage and inventory. Time improves the Tuscan wine quality. At the right moment the wines are then labeled, put into distribution or used for in-house consumption and enjoyed by the drinking/consuming public worldwide.

All tasks are performed personally by the winemaker or at least overseen by the winemaker. Ivan and his team believe that it is very important to maintain direct control of what happens in all stages of their production to each and every bottle of wine produced.

Understanding the path to Tuscany, the origin of the winery, unique stories and approaches is the basis of professional and personal philosophies that evolve with and by the owner, family and workers of La Matteraia.

Ivan clearly states that his family traditions and culture led him to state publicly to his team and customers to "work well and don't stop learning and growing." This is furthered by his admonition to "believe always in what you do." This may sound like common sense for any business but for the owner to publicly talk about it and blend it into work practices elevates them to a high level of output. He seeks an even higher level of output with a goal to triple current production in terms of number of bottles produced.

When asking any business to describe what they do and for whom, many ramble, many stray from the exact question and people come away, not always knowing about the business. Ivan is different. He is very succinct in his summary for La Matteraia:

"I am Ivan Malpaga and my wines are born from my passion. I grew up in my grandfather Isaac's wine cellars where as a child I wandered among full vats of wine. This tradition that is told in the mountains of Trentino is destined to continue its intense history in the Tuscan hills, with desire, where in 1973 my father bought this company."

In 2010, Ivan began to weave the history and his memories culminating in achieving his dream of opening a winery as his grandfather did, aware of the important past behind him and sure of and passionate of future expectations.

The choice of being followed by a true oenologist was fundamental to ensure the high quality of wines that exist from La Matteraia today.

The history was born in the vineyard of expert hands and grows between research, dedication and small gestures of continuous improvement to achieve balance otherwise impossible.

As a concluding note, Ivan offers the suggestion of never just stopping in front of a glorified image of a wine bottle/label or a company logo but learn from the deep story that surrounds the beginning and the path to where the wine has arrived to today. That was his dream, his possibility, and finally his realization that he and others are living today.

MONTEMAGGIO

JUST DOWN A pebble-covered roadway in the municipality of Radda in the province of Sienna in the heart of the Chianti Classico region, is Fattoria di Montemaggio, a fabulous and reputable winery, producing delicious Tuscan wines. This winery is part of over 350 wineries in the Chianti Classico zone of the Tuscany region alone.

This winery is situated where a 14th century tower once stood above an old Roman road that crisscrossed among the hills between Siena and Florence. Many wineries are along this fabled road. By now you have read about the key placement and path of this road between strategic, previously feuding cities. The name, Montemaggio, is derived from "Monte Maggiore" (Big Mountain) symbolizing the elevated location just north of Radda. The vineyard sits high atop rolling hills looking out over what has been mentioned as one of the most striking landscapes visited in the region.

Fattoria di Montemaggio is the result of a dream come true for two dynamic women who are passionate about their craft and visionary in nature. Valeria Zavadnikova is the young owner of the Fattoria, whose passion for wine has compelled her to learn anything and everything about wine, vine growing, and winemaking while transforming this passion into an avid vocation. Ilaria Anichini, is more than Valeria's right arm: She's not only a wine prodigy but a studied agronomist and the director of the winery, having worked at Montemaggio since 2005. Today, she is the manager of the winery. Ilaria, was born and bred in Florence, the place where she studied agronomy at the university with the dream of landing at a place like Montemaggio.

It is not a coincidence then that the image on the logo of Montemaggio is a young Etruscan woman with a basket of grapes on her head.

Note: The Etruscans, were a group of people who settled in Central Italy, credited with founding the wine industry of modern-day Tuscany and having a desire to advance the whole concept and technology of winemaking. The Etruscans took the grapevine introduced and offered by the Greeks, developed it into highly desirable, grape-producing vines, turning out desirable wines for the drinking public.

This very fitting, symbolic logo was the product of the Russian artist Andrey Remnev, a well-known and much appreciated Russian painter, who created the original painting of the Etruscan woman, and his wife, Marina Zimoglyad, who is a designer. The two of them took inspiration from the painting and then created a logo and wine label with the painting as a model.

Before meeting the two women of Montemaggio, let's look a little at the winery itself, the lay of the land, the terroir and process, and the missions and philosophies that surround the management and operations of the winery.

Since 2009, Montemaggio has been a certified organic estate, known for producing pure organic wine. They practice organic agriculture, carrying out cultivation with the maximum respect for nature and the land, without introducing any foreign elements or chemicals that could harm the ecosystem and environment. They term this as being fully connected to the traditions and characteristics of their territory.

All of these traditions, characteristics, practices, and respect translate into a philosophy of producing a very high-quality wine. That philosophy further suggests that the size of the winery stays relatively small in an effort to be able to control every plant, wine, and process component that goes into every bottle produced, sold, and consumed. These 100% handmade wines are very recognizable the minute a bottle is opened. This allows customers to really appreciate the natural taste of the organically produced wine.

Now let's meet the owners.

Valeria Zavadnikova is the owner of Fattoria di Montemaggio. Russian-born and educated in England, Zavadnikova came to Italy with her father and family at the age of 23 with the goal of owning a winery.

She lived in Moscow until the age of 16 and moved to England in order to complete her education. Valeria graduated from both City University London and King's College London with Bachelor in Law and Master in Law degrees respectively.

Her dream of owning a winery was realized at Fattoria di Montemaggio, a diverse wine estate and member of the Consortium of Chianti Classico, and as a self-designated, organic sanctuary of vineyards and olive groves.

Seeing its enormous potential, Valeria threw herself completely into the world of wine, learning as much as she could while studying and working. To further enhance her knowledge, she has completed another Masters in Management and Marketing in the Wine and Spirits sector.

Zavadnikova's business model and vision is positioned around the production of estate-grown, organic, terroir-driven wines. She supplements this identity with the offering of on-site tours, tastings, and experiences including outdoor picnic lunches, cooking classes, painting classes, and villa farmhouse rentals.

Valeria spends her time as owner in the marketing of the brand and identity and everything digital and social media related to the Montemaggio Wine brands.

The second woman behind the success of Montemaggio is Ilaria Anichini , agronomist and estate manager.. Although Ilaria devotes much of her time to grape growing and wine-making, she also participates in promoting the winery's identity in the marketing of the firm. She has been with Montemaggio since 2005.

Note: A viticulturist is someone who studies the practice of growing grape vines while an agronomist studies the science of soil management and crop production.

Ilaria was born and raised in Florence. She grew up loving her city and still does to this day. During her weekends growing up, she would visit all parts of Italy, especially those in the Chianti area. She found herself continuing to return to the Chianti area as she fell more in love with it upon every visit. She is quick to talk about the nature, the wineries, the cellar activity at the wineries, traditional Chianti region life, the smells, pleasant temperatures, sunny days, wine harvests, magical sunsets, and more, that touches all of the senses. Add to this the lush and green hills of Tuscany's heartland, and you can understand why Ilaria fell in love with the region.

All of this drove her to study as an agronomist with a specialization in viticulture and winemaking. Fast forwarding to today, working, she applies her education and experience in a place that she simply describes as amazing, at Montemaggio.

Ilaria is also visionary by nature. She talks about many future projects to realize even more potential for the winery. She emphasizes efficiency where every person working there plays an important role, feels their sense of contribution and has the same passion as the owners, a desire for businesses of all types, winery or not.

Ilaria firmly believes and practices continuous improvement for her craft. She feels this is the key feeder for creativity which is a definite need in viticulture for her winery.

Talking to a tried-and-true agronomist like Ilaria is like talking with a winemaking artist. People like Ilaria don't just look at producing bottles for dollars but look at the quality that comes from the land, the vines, and the grapes. This is evident when she extends life in the barrel, sometimes a year longer than profit-oriented, faster-producing wineries. For Ilaria, it is about the wine and only about the wine: It's about making the best wine she can from the vintage, conditions, and elements that the wine gods gave her in a particular year.

As a case in point for Montemaggio, during the harvest, grapes undergo a very strict selection in the vineyards. Once harvested a similar selection process takes place in the winery. Production at Montemaggio is completely hand harvested only when the grapes are fully ripened to the satisfaction of Ilaria. She is quick to explain that the wines are forever connected to the terroir they have been grown on, taking on the spirit and flavor of the land and growth around it.

The wines produced and sold at and from Fattoria di Montemaggio are aged and refined in the bottle for a longer time compared to other similar wines. It is a process that requires a lot of perseverance and endurance, but in the end yields a product with a uniquely authentic Tuscan taste.

Ilaria Anichini is truly nature bound. Her grapes never see artificial irrigation. She uses almost no new oak and woods so as to avoid any interference with the flavor profile of the Montemaggio wines produced.

When their grapes are ready for harvest, they are all hand sorted. Unripe and over-ripe berries are plucked from the clusters and discarded. She and the vineyard workers will go into the vineyards over a period of days and only pick the ripe bunches, leaving the others to hang for a few extra days for the proper degree of ripening.

Throughout our research, interviews, and conversation, we always go back to Italian traditions, mores, and in most cases, the food of the region/country. Wine is made to drink with food. You've heard it here and will hear it more. The wines produced at Montemaggio are definitely made with food in mind. Tannins are balanced accordingly and are evident from the Sangiovese grape but are meant to drink with food. It can almost be said that to Italians, wine is food, too.

One unique characteristic of the winemaking at Montemaggio and Ilaria's approach is her use of her instinct, taste, feel, and soul. For her, wine is about the weather and natural elements the year gave her. She can talk about difficult years and rainy years and the ensuing problems during those years and yields but throws those aside to focus on the next vintage.

Wine runs in Ilaria's blood. When you talk with winemakers in Chianti Classico they talk about the difficulty of the grape, the terroir, how the wine is a reflection of that terroir and all the natural elements around. Sangiovese is not really grown in any other part of the world.

She takes pride in that and uses her artistic talents to paint the best wine picture she can.

After learning about the people, the approaches, the philosophies, and more, you get a sense that you are already tasting the wine. You can visualize the process and certainly see and experience the passion, loud and clear. Now let's look at the winemaker's day and other things about their path to Tuscan winemaking.

As people become busier and are responsible for more activity and as they find less time to complete tasks, they often multitask to get things done. This helps them accomplish more in a shorter timeframe, do more with fewer people, and have a sense of control of all that needs to be done.

Once again when asked about what a typical day of activity consists of the answer comes back multi-faceted. Ilaria states right away in responding to this that not only is she the shepherd of the winemaking and overall task master, she also takes care of and supervises the care of the vineyards, the tastings and even the accounting after her involvement in cellar activities. Somewhere, the title of general manager shows up next to her name. In this case her work epitomizes the title. She truly is a general manager of many, many activities.

Shifting to other daily activities, another day involves tasting each of the tanks of wine processing to check for any adjustments needed or any need of racking the wines. The talented cellar hand, Edoardo Luvisi, performs the chemical analysis of the vats on a regular basis with a check for approval by Ilaria. Together with Edoardo, they taste and check for things like the sulphite balance and make adjustments where necessary.

Edoardo is classified as a cellar hand who is second to none. He is a key part of the Montemaggio team and very much relied upon by others. He is most engaged, passionate, and very knowledgeable about all things wine; just the right type of person to have by your side in wine ownership.

Every day or two, the temperatures of the wines, the humidity, as well as the hygiene of the tanks and cellar are monitored, checked, and maintained.

All of this is the work of the winemaker at Montemaggio. There are also things that pop up that need tending to that are unplanned. That makes the job that much more interesting and dependent on an expert like Ilaria. So, what does a typical day consist of? The answer is clear. There is no typical day.

Regardless of the day's activities, success for the day is always the goal.

Just like daily activity being different every day, the definition of a successful day takes on different meanings.

A great racking of wine is a successful day. Blending tanks for just the right wine definitely makes for a successful day.

When Ilaria speaks of racking the wine, she means much like Wikipedia defines racking the wine: moving wine from one vessel to another. This can be from tank to barrel, barrel to barrel, and barrel to tank. The purpose of this racking is to further clarify the wine by taking the wine out of barrel, cleaning the barrel of the sediment, and then putting the wine back into barrel. Successful racking aids in wine clarification. It discourages the wrong kind of fermentation and other kinds of microbial spoilage within the blends.

Completing the work in the vineyards is also a successful day for Ilaria. Growing grapes of beauty and high quality and then harvesting them at exactly the right time is counted as a very successful day.

Of course, winemaking is the result of a labor of love. That's the crux of the passion that is often associated with each Tuscan winery. At the end of the day or in this case, at the end of the process, success is measured when someone orders the resulting product. The larger the order, the higher the success, at least in the minds of the winemaker and the producers.

It was mentioned earlier that Ilaria does get involved in hosting groups, organizing tours, and providing tastings of their wines. Success in this area is first when the group engages with the winery for all of this but also when they leave pleased, enthusiastic, wanting more, and tell any and all that are interested in their reviews.

This success is translated even internationally. She and Valeria have traveled the world to introduce the Montemaggio wines outside the borders of Italy including Denmark and Russia in recent times.

In summary, Ilaria classifies her success and the winery's success as one of a successful problem-solving effort. They view themselves as good problem solvers because they do not always jump to the obvious solutions for situations that arise, but they explore other possible ways or more than one solution always looking for new creative, unique, and productive ways to address problems.

BATZELLA

THROUGHOUT THE TOUR of Tuscan winemakers there are many stories about families and generations of estate owners that lead to today's Tuscan winery ownership and operation, not to mention tradition and legacy. Many of the stories are similar with the family component but not all are.

Batzella is a winery actually in the heart of the Bolgheri DOC halfway between the villages of Bolgheri and Castagneto Carducci in an area called Località Badia. The area is known as Badia because in ancient times there was a Camaldolese monastery with a church, cemetery, and extensive religious properties, known as the Abbey of Santa Maria. The wine estate is close to the location of the ancient Badia Santa Maria in Aschis and its church, all but now disappeared.

The Batzella wine estate is located on the central coast of Tuscany. When the owners made their leap of faith into the wine business, they committed themselves to making elegant and genuine wines "with a personality that best expresses the character of this part of the Tuscan territory." Not many Tuscan winemakers use the term "elegant" when describing their wines, but at Batzella they do.

Batzella is considered a boutique family-run winery estate, founded in 2000 when Franco Batzella and his wife Khanh took early retirement from their careers at the World Bank to start a life changing voyage: to make the best "terroir" wine in Tuscany. They even classify their move as a bold, almost crazy undertaking. It was at that time of their retirement that they made the decision to live a dream and make wine in Tuscany.

Khanh was in her early 50s and was looking at her life's direction. She contemplated continuing her career in world finance or making a change, a drastic, unrelated change. With her decision made, she went back to school at the University of Milan to get a special master's degree in vineyard/winery management. Attending school at this point in life put her in a senior position with fellow classmates, almost of mother-like quality. Students of a younger generation with eager energy sat side by side with her during their studies.

During that same time, she had to take the public exam in Siena to become a qualified professional farmer. When finally, her husband finished his consulting job with the Italian Ministry of Finance in Rome in 2004, and with the same desire for a career/life change, he also applied to become a professional farmer. Franco was asked the key question at the time of application which was, "Do you have any farming experience?" Franco's creative, yet truthful reply was "Yes, for three years I assisted my wife who is a professional farmer." The public exam agency replied favorably and stated, "Ah good, then you are qualified with no further need to take the exam." Although qualified, taking actual exams was stressful and difficult for a foreigner. Khanh learned quickly and had a successful start. Their lesson from this was when you need to, you learn quickly, even if you are older or on a new path.

Since the beginning, the owners did all winemaking operations themselves. They were basically learning it one day and teaching their staff the next. With only one full time worker, they hired temporary workers for the busy harvest time. The two owners were waking up in the middle of the night to rack the tanks under fermentation. Racking normally takes several hours to clean the equipment before and after use, in addition to about 20-30 minutes of pumping over the wine from each fermenting tank. Franco did not like having to wake up in the early morning hours to do this work, something they discussed in those early hours of the morning, him sitting on top of the tanks, Khanh at ground level manning the pumps and opening/closing the tank faucets. At that early time of the winery, all the tanks were in open air in the middle of the olive grove because the permit to build a winery building took a long time for approval by local government. It was tough making wine like that under the Tuscan sun. They needed to get creative to keep the tanks cool, using a special cooling system for each tank and supplementing it by running well water over the tanks. It was hard work, but they persisted and made their first wines, all with raving reviews. That's how they started their real wine life.

While many of our Tuscan winemaker stories involve families and multi-generations, Batzella is different. Franco and Khanh's two children are not involved in the wine operation because when Khanh and Franco started their wine life their children already had their own professional careers and passions. They do, however, love to drink the wines produced.

Owners Khanh and Franco continue their wine's description and approach by stating, "We're trying to do something different and in a different way, but always in tune with our land and its traditions."

Following their motto, Quaerendo invenietis (keep searching and you will find), they have combined their passion for perfection with the best wine management practices of today and yesterday (training at the University of California at Davis and at the University of Milan) to make wines that express the typicality of their territory.

In short, a constant commitment to grasp and give voice to their location's distinctive atmosphere and spirit of the land through the grapes is their mission.

These philosophies and beliefs will become more evident as we explore their traditions, culture, and grape varieties used in their wine production.

Batzella Winery produces award-winning Bolgheri DOC wines that are hand-crafted and made to offer the best of the West Coast of Tuscany terroir and personality.

In the U.S., the term "artisanal" comes to mind.

Batzella has always given a distinct personality to its wines in a zone where diversity is hard to find. It is a winery that refuses to get into the wild race for star-studded prices, a trend observed for many Bolgheri wines.

The winery is not in the traditional wine region of Tuscany, Chianti Classico, but in the village of Bolgheri located close to Tuscany's Mediterranean coastline in the northwestern part of the region.

To think that there is a relatively new wine zone or at least a younger zone, in an ancient country is almost unfathomable but that is exactly what you get with the Bolgheri region.

It was a surprise that the fertile, clay like, and sandy soils would be so conducive to grapevine cultivation—and not just any vines and grapes, but those of French varieties.

Bolgheri wines are famous for expressing terroir. The proximity of the sea is one of the place's defining characteristics. The land basks in ample light from the sun and its brilliant reflections off the ocean, enjoys fabulous coastal weather, and is kissed by a sea breeze that ventilates the vines and mitigates the temperatures. Vineyards are compressed in between lush hillsides and early olive groves. Soils are rich in minerals, sand, limestone, clay, and volcanic rock. This sun and seaside influence can be found in the strong and powerful red wines.

The town of Bolgheri is a charming medieval village that rose up around a medieval castle.

The first thing that will strike you is the famous Viale dei Cipressi, or Cypress Avenue, a straight road about three miles long, lined with tall, majestic, centuries-old cypresses that shade the road and lead straight to the Castle of Bolgheri.

Beyond its ancient town walls is an area of Tuscany that feels like a step back in time, a small oasis of Tuscan allure and aristocratic appeal. The town is dotted with shops and restaurants, neat and well-tended, an assortment of old churches and is entirely pedestrian.

Cruising along the Livorno coast you find small, excellent vineyards in the Bolgheri zone.

This is mainly thanks to the sub-zone of Sassicaia, where farsighted bets were placed on Cabernet Sauvignon, which is one of the prestigious reds whose introduction generated a positive trend in wine production harmonizing tradition and novelty.

The small Tuscan town of Bolgheri historically produced simple wines made from the native grapes Sangiovese and Trebbiano.

Though Cabernet Sauvignon was planted in the region in the 1940s, it wasn't until 1994 that the region received DOC status where Super Tuscan wines (Bordeaux reds and Sangiovese) seized center stage.

Now here's a twist. Most of what is written about here is in regard to Italian grapes. After all, it is a book about Tuscan winemaking. While the grapes for Bolgheri grow in Italy, all the vines in the Batzella vineyard come from a specialized nursery in France. Five different clones of Cabernet Sauvignon optimize aromas, bouquets, and provide a unique complexity in the wines produced.

For Batzella, wine is made first of all in the vineyard with the best grapes possible. Cabernets in Bolgheri are capable of giving great wines with a character deeply linked to soil and climate of the territory from which they come, wines that are by no means standardized and globalized but which offer that original elegance with the unrepeatable Mediterranean expression that identifies them from its Atlantic cousins in Bordeaux.

It's interesting that although we talk about Tuscany as an important Italian region, there are many sub-regions and cities and towns, like Bolgheri that pop up throughout the land to make it more diverse than first thought.

Usually, any reference to wine in Tuscany, suggests the Sangiovese grape. Sangiovese is a red fruit that is distinguished by smooth tannins with a memorable character and solid texture, Sangiovese is usually known for its earthy bouquets, currants, black cherries, and hints of undergrowth, plums and even tobacco. In order to talk about the complexity of the Sangiovese grape, it is necessary to talk about the history of the territory where it is grown—Tuscany. This is a land which has produced some of the best wines in the world: Chianti Classico, Nobile di Montepulciano, Brunello di Montalcino.

Sangiovese is the king of grapes, but you cannot talk about Tuscan grapes without talking about other Tuscan grape varieties that are native to the territory. Cabernet Sauvignon is a red berry from the Médoc region of France and just south of Bordeaux. This vine can also be found along these slopes of central Italy thanks to this area's climate which is not too cold in the winter and not too hot in the summer, as well as for its soil which is clayey and stony.

The Bolgheri Region owes its current success to a winemaker named Marchese Incisa della Rocchetta, who in the 1940s made the decision to plant Cabernet Sauvignon on the San Guido estate in an attempt to replicate the Cabernet Sauvignon wines of the Médoc region that he loved.

He and his family drank the wine as their personal *vino da tavola* for years, and it only went on the market as the first Bolgheri wine in 1968. A critic dubbed it a Super Tuscan—yet another punchy name—and this nickname stuck. This introduction generated a positive trend in Tuscany wine production, harmonizing tradition and novelty.

The distinctiveness of this winery is the inevitable result of the uniqueness of the couple who are owners and their many exceptional approaches, daily activities, successes, and philosophies.

While daily activities vary from day to day and season to season, Khanh and Franco talk about their activities as a team and/or couple.

What activities does a typical day consist of?

"We are a team of husband and wife (Franco and Khanh) and one young man working both in the vineyards and the winery. We work mostly with our hands. A day's work depends on the season. In spring our activity mostly takes place in the vineyards, trimming and deleafing. In summer it is mixed with work in the vineyards like trimming the vines with tractor-like equipment and spraying with natural products that ensure no mildew diseases. Activity also takes place in the winery: tasting and taking care of the wines being aged, bottling of wines, labeling and preparing wine orders for customers."

Franco Batzella focuses on marketing, wine promotion and hospitality, while Khanh Nguyen is responsible for production (management of the vineyards and wines in the cellar).

Alessandro Bugnar has worked at Batzella since their first harvest in 2003 when he was just 19 years old.

For operations where timeliness is important, they are helped by a team of additional hands (young and old) who return to the company year after year. Some of them have worked at Batzella since the first harvest in 2003 so they know the vines and the wines and the processes. For them, their job is not considered work. It's a continuous interest, a passion.

These workers have been able to fit into the

Batzella wine family; each of them shares a feeling of being a part of complete ownership of the wines that come from the vineyards. The Batzellas consider themselves lucky in having chosen the right collaborators from early on and instilling in them the same passion as they have along with a culture of discipline and perseverance as they focus on each and every detail of winemaking.

The Batzellas instill a team culture in just about everything they do. They truly know that two people alone cannot run and manage a winery.

They sum up their approach by this quote by Francis of Assisi:

"Whoever works with his hands is a worker

He who works with his hands and his head is a craftsman

He who works with his hands, his head, and his heart is an artist."

You have the vines, the fruit, the soil, the climate, and more but the earth alone is not enough. The owners stated that the best wine is obtained by paying the utmost attention to detail in the vineyard and in the cellar, all together.

In this way each variety from each plot of the vineyard is cared for according to its own needs, and the grapes are harvested at the right moment of their maturity.

They are then vinified and aged until they are ready for blending and bottling. This means thousands of small, detailed activities, some simple, others complex but all require the right know how, care, and attention.

To contribute to the quality of Batzella wine, then, each of the team must want and know how to combine passion with competence, intuition with dedication. In short, they have to work with their hands, their head and their heart: They have to be artists.

To promote this spirit, the winery carries out continuous training to deepen knowledge, update techniques, and increase sensitivity towards wine.

Before we get to what success means to Batzella, there is no winery in Tuscany that is without challenges, problems, and issues that crop up and need tended to.

In every vineyard there are challenges. There are common ones that show up in all vineyards and there are challenges unique to each and every vineyard.

- In the vineyards, one main goal and challenge is to keep the vines and grapes healthy and coach, prod, and nurture them toward maturity using little or no chemical treatment along the way. No chemicals are used to remove weeds as this work is done by hand. Additionally, greens and flowers are planted between the rows in order to encourage development of fauna and microbio in soils, helping the growth of the vineyard. Vine health is further challenged by the unpredictable effects of changing climate conditions throughout the growing season.

- In the winery with grapes of excellent maturity, the intent is to minimize interventions in order to express and preserve the original tastes and characters of the grapes, the land, their passions, and their souls. Here, the quality of the wine goes hand in hand with its personality and elegance, two adjectives not talked much about in Tuscan wineries but very much elaborated upon at Batzella.

- Another big challenge is marketing for a small producer like Batzella. Wine consumers still are very influenced by reputation and prestige. Even with top quality products,

selling requires combining and
delivering the right taste while
getting known wine critics and
influencers to promote the wines.

Batzella puts an emphasis on remaining small as they feel this allows them to make wine in their own way and not be enslaved by the market. The owners choose to not turn their wines into prestige wines whose rarity (either because quantity is extremely limited or price is outrageously high) makes them famous cult wines. That boils down to selling at prices that give fair quality values in the eyes of consumers. Although it is a constant part of winemaking and wine selling, selling with quality appealing to their captive markets contributes to their success.

So we now know more about Batzella. They are successful in all that they do. When asked what a successful day is in their process, they reply:

"When we efficiently finish what we start because in vine growing and winemaking, timing is of utmost importance whether solving problems, avoiding issues, or moving the product to the steps of the winemaking process, all the way through."

In their unique way, the Batzellas recently celebrated 20 years of business. Their individuality was demonstrated by likening their winemaking to music and the conducting of an orchestra. The 20-year celebratory video shows Khanh doing an imaginary orchestral conduction of the Tuscan countryside and winery.

Khanh states in her own musical analogy, that winemaking is like making music and conducting an orchestra. That orchestra is composed of nature, weather, soils, plants, people, and technology, all on the way to the finished drinking product. After seeing this video, so many professionals and amateurs alike remember Batzella and hold the analogy as very interesting, even intriguing.

The Batzellas state that "Making wine is making music. Like music, wine gives so many the opportunity to experience emotions while making it and drinking it."

The orchestra analogy comes in to play by describing the various orchestral components:

"The working hands are like the musicians. The vines are like the instruments that respond to the musicians' expertise and also their passions.

The terroir is like the concert hall, more or less capable, acoustically.

The weather, with more or less sun and various unpredictability, is like the listening public who react to the music with more or less warmth and emotions."

After blending and storage the wine moves on to tasting. Khanh concludes her analogy by stating that, "If it is good wine, we know we made good music."

The Batzellas feel the Goldberg Variations of Bach, for instance, represent well the emotions felt when making wine.

All of the steps of winemaking evolve around the same melody but play out in so many different ways. That makes every crop and every vintage different.

If you want to experience the music and orchestra analogy, take a look at the steel musician statue at the entrance to the vineyard.

While many philosophies and approaches come forth from Batzella and its unique owners, they often offer simple words of wisdom for consumers: Trust your own taste and be adventurous.

BECONCINI

THERE IS A notion in the world of business that those that are successful work on the business, not in the business. While the information presented here is related to the lives of Tuscan winemakers, their jobs, daily activities and more, they still have a business to be responsible for. We are trying to outline and highlight all of those described activities but there are unique instances where one stands above the rest in a certain area. Agricola Pietro Beconcini is one of those.

Agricola Pietro Beconcini is one of the better examples where the winemaker proprietor is working on the business more than in the business. You will see that in action here as you see activity related to business design, execution, and planning, much like any other successful business, more so than descriptions of daily activity and the day in the life of a Tuscan winemaker.

When hearing or talking about Chianti wine, tried and true stories arise referring to the location of the vineyards, lush rolling hills, art and architecture reflective of medieval periods, and a location along the famed Via Francigena. The town of San Miniato, its geography, surroundings and its wines, is no different.

San Miniato is a small town lying on the outskirts of Pisa, actually between Pisa and Florence, in Tuscany and home to the historical Agricola Pietro Beconcini. Many describe the San Miniato area as the Tuscan town that has everything of the Italian way of life and dream, including beautiful countryside views, the always mentioned rolling hills, and the many Tuscany wines at hand.

San Miniato is on Via Francigena, which in medieval times was the main connecting route between northern Europe (Canterbury, England to be exact) and Rome. Because of this, San Miniato had a constant flow of friendly compatriots and hostile warriors, traders of all goods and services, travelers from near and far, and a flood of religious pilgrims making the pilgrimage to Rome.

The winery in this famed region is Agricola Pietro Beconcini, a fourth generation estate, owned by Leonardo Beconcini and his partner, Eva Bellagamba.

In the 1950s, Leonardo's grandfather, Pietro Beconcini, who had been a sharecropper on the land that was then owned by the Marchesi Ridolfi family purchased the property. The grandfather's original goal was to dedicate the land to local sharecropping. At the time, the farm was complete and chock-full with grains, beans, grape vines, olive trees, and forest land. Leonardo's father dedicated his energies to transitioning the land to solely producing wine.

In the 90s, Leonardo took control of the estate and has taken that passion and heritage forward, producing and offering the highest quality of wines from San Miniato and known all around Tuscany, Italy, and the world.

Leonardo Beconcini's work and path to winemaking took a deliberate pace starting in the early 1990s when he took over the reins of the business from his father. In 1997, Leonardo was joined by his colleague and companion, Eva Bellagamba. Eva has a similar vision and passion and made the decision to share in the winemaking and business building efforts of Leonardo, foregoing her earlier desired future of becoming an architect.

Leonardo is quick to cite personal and even professional qualities that are all key to his success, work, and business. He talks of his patience and even cites caution as two of those qualities. He extends these to what really is his "chronological" recipe for his wine business:

- Coming into lands that were traditionally worked as farmland, Leonardo works hard to have an in-depth understanding of what is now vineyards and the effect of that land on grape production.

- Selecting the right grape clones for future grape production and eventual wine production. In Leonardo's case he was very careful to select two local Sangiovese clones. He guesses that it took nearly four years to reach his selection of clones. He still works with them today, because he feels they respond best to his desire to progress his grape production and winemaking from producing straightforward wines to a Sangiovese grape capable of yielding long-lived, desirable, complex wines.

- Those clones are still used today for wine production. Leonardo's search for the right version that

fit the terroir of the vineyard
to produce the right wine was
all part of his research and
subsequent cloning of exactly the
grape he wanted.

Note about clones:

A clone, in the world of grapevines (from the Greek word for twig) is a genetically distinct sub-type of a grape variety created by taking cuttings, also known as graftings, from an original "mother" vine with desirable characteristics and reproducing new, identical vines of the exact same qualities and characteristics.

- Leonardo's decision to increase plantings of the Malvasia Nera grape (often used and blended with the Sangiovese grape). Malvasia Nera wines are used for blending because of its strong aroma and dark color, popularly planted in Tuscany, especially in early Tuscan times.

- Leonardo's final recipe component is the discovery of the San Miniato grape variety that is now known as Tempranillo.

Leonardo Beconcini, proprietor was learning and experimenting with the right vines to use in his wine production. When Leonardo took over as winemaker he selected the best grape producing vines and started replanting and cultivating ungrafted vines; the same vines that survived diseases that hit many of Europe's vines. Although Sangiovese had been his main target, a few years later Leonardo also became interested in some of these older, other vines.

There were old, old vines mixed with others. Upon intensive research by Leonardo and micro-vinification (according to Wikipedia, a winemaking technique used often for experimental batches of wine where the wine is fermented in small, specialized vats), on some of the vines he discovered a vine that intrigued him. These vines produced excellent grapes, but nobody knew what grape it was. As time went on, Leonardo had amassed many hectares of vineyards of the unknown grape.

For a long time, the identity and origin of this vine remained a mystery to Leonardo. It was at that point that the family had them tested using "plant DNA" testing. The testing eventually showed the old vines to be Tempranillo vines: wines and grapes of Spanish descent, predominantly grown in Spain and used to make full bodied red wines. It was very unusual to find them growing in Italy. Cuttings from these old vines were planted, nurtured and grown to be used in the Beconcini wines of today.

Leonardo, upon learning the results of the plant DNA testing remarked,

"I was both fulfilled and very surprised. In fact I was thinking we were cultivating a traditional, indigenous vine of some sort on the way to extinction. But we were in front of a centuries old grape variety that arrived from Spain and the deepest, rich, past of San Miniato."

As mentioned, this is not a primer on Italian grapes or Italian wines for that matter. It is about the lives of winemakers and the surroundings of "their story" to understand what they get up to do every day along with their vision.

Because of that we are not here to talk about particular grapes within the Chianti region. However the Beconcini Tempranillo is one grape worth talking about because of its uniqueness, history, and resulting Tuscan wine product produced from this grape.

The reason it is worth a mention here is because of the fascinating history of its path to Tuscany wines, old and new.

Beconcini lays claim to being the only producer of Tuscany wines made from the Tempranillo grape. There is lots of history that backs this claim as it is deep in old world lore, Italian tradition, Tuscan culture, and stories of heritage.

The Tempranillo grape is a famous, primary

red grape, originally from Spain and now respon-sible for the worldly red wines from Ribera del Duero and Rioja, Spain, the regions of Spain pro-ducing some of the most complex and flavorful red wines in that country. Tempranillo has been known as the backbone of Spain's notable wine region, Rioja, for many generations. Often made and blended with other local grapes Garnacha (Grenache) and Mazuela (Carignan), Rioja reds have been Spain's signature wine for centuries.

How did a Spanish grape for winemaking end up in the land of Tuscany, over a thousand miles away?

The answer has been mentioned here and spoken about many times: the ancient Via Franci-gena. This famous roadway and thoroughfare passes directly through the present day Beconcini wine estate, alongside the very vineyards that pro-vide the Tempranillo grape for Beconcini's wine.

Religious pilgrims and other travelers passed through, starting from points across northern Europe heading to Rome, via two main routes: the Via Francigena which originated in Canter-bury, England and Santiago di Compostela, orig-inating in Spain. At the time, religious leaders, travelers, and pilgrim organizers, in addition to their religious duties, missions, and congrega-tion leadership, were also responsible for over-seeing agricultural and farming undertakings to provide for their followers.

New vineyards were started in those days, along the way, by planting grape seeds all along their routes of travel. Seed planting was used most, primarily due to the fact that over long journeys and pilgrimages it was easier to carry small containers of seeds rather than larger, heavy bundles of actual vine cuttings. Thus, seeds were left and planted in Tuscany and other areas along the way.

That is how the Tempranillo grape found its way to Tuscany.

Matthew Callcott-Stevens, writer and friend of the Beconcinis states, "The variety that was once unaccepted in the land of Chianti now grows strong all thanks to the hard work and dedication of Leonardo Beconcini. Tempranillo was made known by the Riojans and mastered by the Beconcinis in Tuscany."

Being the passionate winemaker that he is, Leonardo feels that there is even more potential in the grapes he is working with, given the terroir and winemaking process. His vision is that he will always be a continuous learner in this area and may find newer and better grape production maintaining a high degree of uniqueness and originality.

Leonardo talks much about the Beconcini family philosophy of life and wine growing and extends this by stating that his most representative wine is influenced by his terroir and his "production philosophy." He strives to produce the best possible cultivation of his vineyards in the satisfaction of many different markets and wine delivery. In other words, he truly does take pride in demonstrating the greatness and versatility of the Sangiovese grapes of his Tuscany lands in the area near San Miniato for many to enjoy.

As we leave Beconcini, Leonardo leaves us with "We're working on a few new wines. Today we have the satisfaction to have realized the dream of producing two unique Tempranillo wines in Tuscany. We work simply like a good farmer, with the maximum respect for the Tuscan tradition and the old, vacated vineyards (that can reveal unexpected surprises). Most of all, we never get distracted from our traditional, Sangiovese based wines; a Sangiovese that is our particular terroir and expresses something very special and unique.

We are an artisanal family-owned winery for many generations, and we will continue to explain our wines by travelling around the world and organizing tastings with our selected importers, who prefer to work with small wine realities like us.

As it is said, "It's a great value that what you taste when you drink our wines is that which our soul expresses. We put that front and center."

VILLA CALCINAIA

SINCE THIS BOOK is about the life of Tuscan winemakers, we really wanted to concentrate on what the actual winemakers do on a daily basis, what their activity consists of from start to finish, and the many steps of the winemaking process that they are involved in. As we dove deep into this, we found many unique things about each winemaker interviewed. It is worth sharing some of those along with the daily activity descriptions. This quality of uniqueness couldn't be better illustrated than our dive into Villa Calcinaia.

You will even learn how the family Capponi actually stopped the French King from invading Italy during warring Renaissance times.

Let's look at the character of this winery as well as the winemaker's daily activity.

Villa Calcinaia is a wine estate situated in the center of the Chianti Classico area near the town of Greve-in-Chianti. This historic estate has been home to the Capponi family since 1524 and is maintained by Count Sebastiano Capponi and his brother Niccolò. Villa Calcinaia is known for Chianti Classico wines.

Calcinaia is the heart of the Capponi family estate with each generation giving new life to the land, fields, woods, olive groves, vineyards, cellars, and final wine product left before them. Throughout the investigation and exploration of Villa Calcinaia you find wines produced that reflect the passion the family has for the lands they are part of. It's interesting to hear the descriptions they associate with every vintage. They will state very clearly that they share the hopes, worries, pride, and care that come with making honest wines. You usually don't hear these descriptors from a Tuscan winemaker. All of this passion extends to their philosophy, stated as, "Love for the land, respect for tradition, and the rightful pride in bearing the name of Capponi."

Even though there is a long and glorified history associated with this estate, the family has still made many investments in winemaking technology to improve their production and make the best wines of the region.

Count Sebastiano Capponi, the 20th generation of the Capponi family, runs the estate of

Villa Calcinaia. Yes, he's a real count, and also a Knight of St. Stephen, a Roman Catholic Tuscan dynastic military order founded in the mid 1500s. The order was created by Cosimo I de' Medici, then first Grand Duke of Tuscany, and a medal-holder of The Sovereign Military Order of Malta, a Catholic lay religious order, traditionally of a military, chivalric, and noble nature.

Sebastiano Capponi is a down-to-earth, enthusiastic winery director. Many classify him as having a larger-than-life presence. He is an educated, logical, critical thinker. When his schedule allows, he still loves to personally take his guests on a tour of the estate to give them an overview of the family history, the grounds, and the authentic wine production which is in continuous improvement and experimentation, as he describes it. Some have even gone as far as to classify him as the Chianti Classico Renaissance man.

Historically, the Capponis were involved in the popular Florentine trades of silk and wool, and soon moved into banking. You could call them enterprising merchants, entrepreneurs, and just good businesspeople for that time. In fact, moving into the banking business allowed the family to start buying properties all over Europe. Villa Calcinaia was purchased in one of those instances.

The acquisition of the wine estate in 1524 provides an anchor in the colorful history of the Capponi family of Florence. They have ancestors who were instrumental in stopping the French King from invading Italy.

While this book is about the life of the winemakers, as we have said, there are many unique story lines, instances, experiences, and offerings of all we interviewed. Some stories are worthy of recounting here.

The colorful history just mentioned is exemplified by the story of one of the Capponis preventing war with France. Back in the late 1490s, the king of France was venturing to Naples and had a notion to stop in Florence. While there he decided to lay siege to the city of Florence. This was done usually to extract money out of the city, not necessarily for a true conquering of the land. The king asked Piero Capponi, the prime minister of Florence at the time, for a ransom. Refusing to "counteroffer" the ransom demand, the king fumed. His exact words were, "Well, if that's your final word, we're going to blow our trumpets and invade the city. The senior Capponi replied with, "If you're going to blow your trumpets, we're going to toll our bells and call the population to defend the city." Piero Capponi from then on was known as Peter of the Bells. The statue of Peter is located in the Gallery of the Uffizi amongst the four defenders of Florence. These are the only statues in the Gallery that face the Arno River. The episode became very popular during the reunification of Italy standing as an example of how Italians fight for their homeland.

Sebastiano relays more history as he describes the fact that the family has been making wine since 1524. A favorite quote and one that we hear from many Tuscan winemakers is that, "Wine is part of the diet." Especially Tuscan wines which pair perfectly with food.

In another recent interview, Count Sebastiano outlines his philosophy of winemaking. Understanding these philosophies is important as we learn and understand all we can about the life of a Tuscan winemaker.

Sebastiano runs his winery with many philosophies. Some are very traditional and family based, others are a result of today's times, his continuous learning, and application to continue a legacy of quality wines.

Even in casual conversation he will let out a philosophical nugget. In a recent interview he stated, "Quality is a necessary condition and goal but not sufficient. The goal is to make distinctive wines."

Sebastiano's main philosophy of winemaking is to let the good continue and if the good is no longer good, fix it. As organic farmers, they are not dependent on chemicals and fertilizers. If problems arise because of this, the winery's innovativeness steps in and solves the problems. He often lets nature take its course rather than undertaking lots of pump overs and racking. He strongly feels that nature knows better what to do and he just intervenes if there is a problem or things don't go as planned.

His philosophy continues into his thoughts on being an organic farmer. He wants to live in a place that is as healthy as possible. That is one important aspect of making organic wines. He strives to leave a legacy for his kids, grandkids and the next generations that is healthy and clean. Ruined and contaminated soil is not part of that. Preservation of what is present along with an attitude of always improving the state and conditions wins out in this respect.

Still, overall, the estate comes back to the philosophy of "Love for the land, respect for tradition, and the rightful pride in bearing the name of Capponi."

Hospitality is the hallmark of *Villa Calcinaia*, paired with *organic* farming and the traditions stated in their philosophy statement.

A note on organic viticulture and organic farming:

Organic vineyards focus on the growth of the healthiest vine, a vine that can withstand pests of all types and sustain themselves naturally.

This means developing healthy soils and a balanced ecosystem within the vineyard system. It also means a lot of work devoted to the healthy side of the whole process. Mostly this means not using fertilizers and pesticides that non-organic vine growers use.

A wine and grape that has a designation of being "organically-grown" means that no pesticides or synthetic chemical applications were used in the vineyard. Organic wines have to be made solely with organic grapes without the addition of non-organic elements during the winemaking process.

Organic farming has been the standard at Villa Calcinaia since Sebastiano took over the estate's management in 1992. The farm was certified in the year 2000 and the winemaking was certified as being produced with organic grapes since the 2014 vintage and is labeled as such. Organic farming helps to preserve the health of the vines and protect the natural environment of the region.

Since Sebastiano took over the reins of the estate's winemaking management, there has been an appreciable rise in the quality of the wines, with the switch to organic viticulture being a major contributor to this.

On to a typical day for this Tuscan winemaker. What's that? A typical day? There is no such thing.

When asked to describe a typical day as a winemaker and estate manager/owner, what answer do you think Sebastiano gave? By now you have heard others answer this question and the answers have been unanimous in reply. There is no typical day; every day's activity is different. He likes the diversity of his work, especially being an integrated farm. Not only is there the management of the wine production but there also is olive oil production, animal herding, goat cheese production, and other products and outputs of nature all in addition to building restoration, maintenance, and management.

Before the COVID pandemic of 2020, Sebastiano's time was mostly spent traveling the world, marketing and selling the wines of Villa Calcinaia. Of course, he is responsible for everything going on at the winery, much like the entrepreneur of any business venture.

When traveling, Sebastiano has a great ability to delegate to his cellar master, Sabrina. He suggests that they operate as a married couple. She is present on the premises every day and when need be, she and Sebastiano discuss the issues, problems, and opportunities that present themselves on a daily basis.

Sebastiano likes the diversity of activity beyond what has so far been described. He likes doing a bit of everything but looks forward to getting back to more world traveling to market his company and products.

For the first 10 of the past 21 years, Sebastiano was involved almost entirely in the production end of the business. He built up processes and standards to the point that he could eventually take off on travels. He has cultivated a very high trust factor so that his strength of delegation can come forward.

His intellectual background and his heritage is ingrained in his work ethic and beliefs.

It is always a pleasure to ask successful people for words of advice, especially for others that want to get into the same business or to prosper in the same business. A lasting word of advice from Sebastiano that is a common theme among many Tuscan winemakers is that winemaking and estate management is hard work. We have written about the fact that it is not all romance and tasting.

The perceived romance of wine might draw people into the winemaking vocation, but, as many Tuscan winemakers will attest, the job isn't all that glamorous. It demands long days, scientific knowledge and practicality, patience of and the ability to handle Mother Nature, attention to detail, devotion to cleanliness and production standards, a wide network if involved in branding, marketing and sales, and just plain hard work as described.

Italy is beautiful and it can remain beautiful in your work if you don't have to deal with the state, the public, the laws and regulations that are all outside of winemaking but part of winery ownership. That's not to say don't follow your passion. If you have a passion to make wine and manage an estate, do it but realize that it is hard work, not always glamorous and easy going.

The problems that crop up in estate management are generally related to weather and nature. In the last few years there has been scarce grape production due to warming and late frost. Mild winters and an early spring contribute to this late frost. Late frost is damaging to grape crops. Because of their location in the valley and the fact that water on the opposite side of the valley runs underground, the cold currents come to his side. Hot summers that damage grape integrity further contribute to a suffering grape crop. They do have innovations to help manage this related to later pruning, shadowing, and more.

When asking Sebastiano what his favorite wine is, his response is his favorite wine is his most important wine. Of course, this is also a business-oriented answer, as his most important wine is the wine that gets him business and grows his business. In the case of Villa Calcinaia, the most important wine to Sebastiano is his own produced Villa Calcinaia Chianti Classico wine.

The importance of this wine to Villa Calcinaia is due to the fact that it is the estate's wine that most people come across first. Sebastiano likened it to a first date. If you like the first date, there will be a second date. If you don't, no more dates. Another analogy that makes sense of this importance is that the Villa Calcinaia Chianti Classico wine is the "calling card" of the winery; the flagship wine representing everything about Villa Calcinaia.

Sebastiano offers that it was a privilege to be relatively small in wine production. In this way, he and the estate can continue to focus on the things they like producing and finding customers that like what they produce. He went so far as to assign the term "elective affinity" to this. That is his core business, and he is privileged to keep it that way in addition to the other philosophies and traditions that he shares.

POLIZIANO

WHERE ELSE IN Tuscany does a family patriarch hand over the ownership of the family wine estate and winery by tossing his son the keys?

When Dino Carletti said "Here, take the keys to the vineyard," his son Federico did not hesitate for a second. He took over the Poliziano vineyards and winery, with those keys in hand. The area was a calm, typical, peaceful Italian village until then. In spite of his quiet demeanor, Federico had big plans for the wines of Montepulciano. Federico finishes this story by stating that the timing was perfect: his father was no longer very interested in winemaking and Federico was ready to take over. Wise man that he is, that's when Dino literally handed over the keys!

Today, Federico runs the Poliziano winery, as one of the most prestigious producers of Vino Nobile di Montepulciano, while simultaneously growing the estate. Federico firmly believes that even at this time, and even at the state that Poliziano is, there is tremendous potential in the wines of Montepulciano.

This wine estate, surrounded by the Tuscan landscape and environment, is halfway between two beautiful and famous Tuscan cities, Montepulciano and Cortona on the slopes near the village of Gracciano. The area is particularly known for its red wines made from the Vino Nobile di Montalcino grapes. On these ridges, at the best altitudes and positions realizing very favorable climates, are the vineyards of Vino Nobile di Montepulciano. The farm is located in Montepulciano Stazione, while the vineyards are situated on the road which leads to the center of Montepulciano from Valiano.

The Poliziano Estate was founded in 1961 by Dino Carletti, and it is still managed today by his family. Dino Carletti was moved by a romantic and passionate vision for his native land and purchased that said land. Today Poliziano has grown and consists of over 500 acres.

Dino Carletti chose the name "Poliziano" for his wine estate/farm because he loved the work of the renowned native poet, Angelo Ambrogini (1454-1494). His nickname, Poliziano, by which he is primarily identified in present day, was derived from the Latin name of his birthplace, Montepulciano (Mons Politianus). He is the most famous Poliziano in Italian history. Ambrogini's portrait hangs in the tasting room in the center of the estate. Polizano's most famous poem, *Le Stanze* figures prominently among Poliziano's wines, primarily as the wine labeled and bottled as Le Stanze.

Ambrogini was an Italian classical scholar, humanist, and poet of the Florentine Renaissance era. His scholarship was instrumental in the separation of Renaissance Latin from medieval norms and for developments and uses in and the study of oral and written historical language sources. Poliziano had a varied history, as he lived and worked under the protection of the Medici in Florence, obtaining through their influence the Chair of Rhetoric and Poetry at the University of Florence.

Federico Carletti is known, and many times referred to, as Signore Poliziano. Like Poliziano, Federico was born in this Montepulciano region. His entire family was from the very same place where he lives now. It's a very rare thing, in this area, to live where you originate, but Federico considers himself very lucky for this. He grew up tending the vines and has a special love for the terroir (land, environment, and surroundings) and "his" land, stating that this is his place of choice for his family and him to live and that there is nowhere else they would rather live.

Federico pursued his agriculture degree in Florence with the intention of carrying on the family winemaking business. After completing his agricultural studies, Federico worked in northern Italy. As Federico gained professional experience in wineries of northern Italy, he had very close dialogue with the producers of Chianti Classico.

In 1980, he returned to his native land of Tuscany and began working full time on his father's wine estate. He implemented significant investments and development strategies for Poliziano wine, which led to the creation of new qualities and a new brand in 1982. This eventually led to the renewal of winemaking techniques, the opening of international markets, and new and more customers.

Federico recalls the story of his very first visit to France and the French vineyards in 1983. He was young and he felt like a pioneer, an up and comer, of wine and winemaking at that time. He knew that in Italy there was much to learn. Gaining the perspective of French winemakers helped him understand what making quality wines was all about, the work involved, the passion, and the resulting successes. He was shocked, surprised, and of a shaken nature. He now defines that realization as one of the most determining experiences in his career. At that point, with that feeling of passion, he came back to Tuscany and worked fanatically to achieve what he witnessed in the French wine regions.

Federico's time in France led to many valuable experiences and stories of his time there. As a result of being in the wine business, Federico had the opportunity to taste a wine while in the company of a famous oenologist. Both were super excited and pleasantly surprised upon the tasting of what they described as a juicy fresh wine. Both were convinced, after the tasting, that the wine just tasted was relatively young—a few years old at the most. As it turned out both had just tasted a very well known, well-aged, Chateaux Figeac 1970.

After taking over the company management, Federico immediately made a professional and philosophical change by studying and working only with grapes owned by him (Estate Winery).

All wines are made from the grapes of Poliziano's own vineyards. They buy no fruit. "I want to make the best wine I can starting from the grapes that I can grow in this region." He thinks that the region's own character or typicity should shine through in the wines. He also prefers 100% control of the grape material. All grapes are harvested by hand. Many separate micro-vineyards of Poliziano are vinified separately and then blended.

Poliziano is also among the wine producers who have reinvented the way they work from base plants and viticultural practices to the work in the cellar. Things like wines being fermented at higher temperatures, using selected yeasts and with pronounced oak character have moved towards fermentation at lower temperatures, with "natural" yeasts and less oak treatment.

From pruning to tying, from the choice of the shoots to the palisade, from the topping to the first selection of the grapes, each step takes place in the expert hands of the Poliziani winemakers, who intervene on the basis of the specific conditions of each plant, each particle, and each vintage. The choice of varietal and planting layouts do not impose themselves on the territory but respect it. All of this attention contributes and enhances the naturalness and terroir of the wine.

Concentrating on quality winemaking, modern, up-to-date technology, applications and processes, and respect for the environment, Federico obtains from the high-density vines a Noble Wine of great depth and quality. Fast forward two decades: Federico has created some of the finest wines in this top-quality wine-producing area.

Federico thinks of himself "in addition to a winemaker and estate owner, as a true farmer." He is "convinced that fine wines originate in the vineyard" and in this case, his. Selected clones, planting layouts, pruning methods and processing systems are chosen with the sole objective of ensuring the quality of the resident and captive grapes. Federico states that, "This is the starting point for my wines: they are made only from grapes grown on the estate, respecting their original vintage and the typicality of the area they come from."

Each of the Poliziano wines is made mainly from these Sangiovese grapes that are referred to as the starting point of their wines. Locally these grapes are called by the historic name of Prugnolo Gentile.

Vino Nobile di Montepulciano is one of Tuscany's most iconic and historic red wines produced. Produced in the eastern part of the Montepulciano region, Vino Nobile di Montepulciano is generally categorized as one of the three great red wines of Tuscany, along with Chianti Classico and Brunello di Montalcino. Understanding these three wines will give you the understanding of most, if not all, of Tuscany winemaking.

The aforementioned Prugnolo Gentile grapes, characterize the Montepulciano area. Winemakers of this region dedicate great attention and care to these grapes because of the full potential available of a territory with a rich Tuscan wine history. The result of this for Poliziano is the wine, Vino Nobile di Montepulciano, balanced with structure, stable, with intense aromatic features that truly represent Tuscany wines.

"At Poliziano, the focus is on uncompromising quality where only the very best fruit to obtain a young, fruity, and full-bodied wine is selected." That is straight from the mouth of Federico Carletti, Winemaker.

By now you have learned enough to characterize a Tuscan winery and Tuscan winemakers. You have also learned that there are differences and nuances for each of these.

Poliziano is another winery with unique characterizations. Let's look at a few of these.

- Poliziano wines bring to mind the tradition and culture of the territory but also have the scope and power to "speak to wine lovers of the world."

- Poliziano lives by the notion of the earliest bond between the land, the people, the culture, traditions, and authenticity.

- The Poliziano company as a whole has grown over the years with what the owners describe as dedication to the land and the craft, the professionalism involved in the business and product production and fortitude. This is all done while

following advanced approaches,
procedures and methodologies
of the cultivation and the
harvest of grapes, along with the
continuance of the science and
study of wine and winemaking,
as it applies to Poliziano.

Now that we understand the character of Po-liziano, let's look at the inner workings and life of this winemaker.

Federico tends to divide his workday day into three parts. The first part is tending to and understanding the state of affairs as it relates to the agronomic conduction of the vines. Federi-co views agronomy much like the standard defi-nition: the science and technology of producing and using plants in agriculture for food, fuel, fiber, recreation, and land restoration. Every-thing that happens at Poliziano is encompassed by this definition.

Federico spends hours and a major part of his workday in the vineyards checking their stage at any point of the year and season.

The second part of his daily activity centers around the oenological area in general; the study and process of winemaking. He is deep inside the winery, involved in tastings, deciding blends and directing storage and bottling all the way to the finished product.

Finally, the rest of his day is related to solving problems, tending to administrative matters and issues that arise almost daily. While previously involved in marketing he is doing more delegation of this so that others can share the same experiences that he has had, in other parts of the country and world.

The successful result of all this is basically accomplishing all that is planned for each day. Add to this constant and bigger orders for product that satisfy their many clients and that is Federico's success.

Every winemaker interviewed has their own personal philosophy. Federico is no different. Simplistically he will state: "Believe and enhance your terroir," which in personal terms is, "Believe and enhance who you and your roots are."

Further lessons and philosophies include always being honest and standing up for what one believes in. That's talked about and widespread at Poliziano.

Professionally, Federico is on a continuous learning path. He promotes to all that they should never stop learning. Nature is continuously changing. One piece of advice which will always be true is that you can never stop learning. Learning opportunities are everywhere, especially if you look for them.

It sounds like common sense or at least like common wine sense but Federico tells all customers and all visitors to their estate that the more you see and taste, the better. There probably are no finer words of wisdom in the wine world.

In Federico's case, his daily work involves his kids. He works with and around them every day. The family passion for wine and the territory continues with Federico's children, Francesco and Maria Stella, who today act as Federico's fundamental advisors to interpret and face current and future financial, planning, and growth challenges. They share new stories every day, joke around, have fun and enjoy their passion, all as a family.

Federico breeds a culture with strong values. Consistency and honesty is at the base of their beliefs and work ethic. They also strongly believe "in what we are, our Nobile and our Montepulciano," and are always humble enough for any criticism, self-doubt, and ready for adjustments to those.

The terroir of this Montepulciano area is what makes the winemaking what it is today for Poliziano. The climate, soils and environment also contribute to the reasons why Sangiovese grows here and not in any other part of the world. The Sangiovese grape is a very hard and yet delicate grape—thick skinned on the outside with a delicate inside. It needs attention and knowledge, much like you have read here.

Looking back, Federico did his humanistic studies in high school which gave him the sensitivity needed to understand cultures and to approach things always with an open mind. His degree in Agronomy influenced his real approach to wine and winemaking. The formal education taught Federico that quality starts in the vineyards with the different soils, treatments and maturations of the grapes having a huge impact on grapes and the final wine product.

Federico always talks about his dad and the influence he had on Federico's upbringing, desires, passions, and path. As his dad bought the first parcel of land to make wine, Federico became more excited about the venture. He was working a distance away in Northern Italy and felt a passionate cry to bring him home. He came home; didn't hesitate and hasn't looked back since.

Federico is happy to talk about his path in Tuscany winemaking and how it has traversed over nearly four decades. He has gone the way from the adoption of international varieties and big oaked wines to the return to traditional Sangiovese and a focus on showcasing the local *terroirs*.

Federico has since built Poliziano into a noted producer with "more than 30 releases scoring 90 points or higher in *Wine Spectator* tastings over the past 20 years."

Federico himself admits that previous Poliziano wines made by his father were thin wines. "The quality was very low." It is gratifying to raise the standard and to see his work recognized.

From the beginning, Federico made his

mark by working only with the ripest, best-quality fruit. "I selected 50 to 60 percent of grapes and the quality changed immediately," he says.

Most Tuscan winemakers will say that grape selection is the most important part of the winemaking process. It remains Federico's obsession. He is determined to keep up with technology for his vineyard and to stay on the edge of production and processing modernization. To this end, he has invested in an expensive sorting system, based in what is known as a modern gravity-fed winery.

However, Federico doesn't use the technology and equipment for his best wines.

"The machines are too brutal, too fast. For our top wines, we use manual selection," says Federico, who helps man the sorting tables during harvest.

Poliziano has some unique techniques, applications, and winemaking methods. They are proud to talk about their 'soft' production. Their techniques and applications are all very soft on the grapes. They do not make use of pumps and they don't want to be harsh on their fruits of the vine at any point in their process. In the vineyard they work "per plot" which allows them to keep track of every parcel of vineyard specifically. This allows for the right treatment at the right time, preventing interruptions like diseases or poor vines that may arise if vines aren't checked or cured in the right way, promptly. This even extends to aging. Their aging is in different dimensions of wood for their Nobiles as they don't want any wood influences interfering with the natural aromas of their Sangiovese grapes and production.

One challenge facing this business just like any other business is fierce competition. Cultural barriers can challenge the worldly wine culture. Most want to compare the culture to that of their homeland. That misunderstanding or lack of understanding is disappointing to any Tuscan winemaker as they love what they do and what they produce for others to enjoy.

Federico loves adding to conversations by talking about his biggest success. He states that after years of chasing modernity, international varieties, and nouvelle cuisines, realizing that going back to his traditions and his culture was the purest and most successful path to passion and success. "It's what I happen to do and enjoy the best."

I GREPPI

TUSCANY WINEMAKING AND the title of this book reminisce about old word wines, winemaking, wine tasting, the evolution of winemaking, and more. In these older countries and regions there usually is not a whole lot of new things to observe, especially as they relate to Tuscan wines. There are exceptions, however, along the way. There are new things that pop up every now and then. I Greppi is one of those wineries that fits that exception. I Greppi represents a new chapter and some new nuances in their production and company. You are about to read that story.

What happens when you take a bunch of scientists, academicians, and visionaries, and introduce them to a vineyard on the Tuscan coast? The answer is the new chapter of the I

Greppi story. The vineyard was created in 2001 by the Cancellieri and Landini families. The production and wine is still overseen today by Alessandro Landini who is part of a Tuscan wine dynasty with generations of experience producing Chianti Classico. Landini continues to serve as a consultant, advisor, and mentor to the current owners. In 2017, after researching Bolgheri's landscape and terroir, a new international group of associates took over the I Greppi brand. With an appreciation of the land and rich environment, the new owners, led by Irish geologist Dr. Neil McMahon, also saw the potential for developing the wines and the vineyard into a world-class product and brand for international markets.

"We are a group of wine lovers, scientists, geologists, economists, and horticulturalists, who think about winemaking differently. Using our expertise, we look to the past, as well as the present and future, so that our wines will be constantly evolving and improving. Our understanding of the rocks and soils, the very basis of terroir, helps us to understand why the Etruscans first developed wine in this region millennia ago. Our viniculture is incorporating the newest scientific techniques and research from the Napa Valley in California, so that our wines will be continually evolving and improving. Together with the vineyard's traditional Italian winemaking heritage, our goal is to make great taste accessible, and share our knowledge and the story behind every bottle."

The estate is a short distance from the picturesque Mediterranean coastline in the sacred homeland of the Super Tuscan movement. I Greppi Vineyard is located in the heart of the Bolgheri DOC area between the villages of Bolgheri and Castagneto Carducci. The word greppo (plural: greppi) means slope in Italian, as in a sloped hillside vineyard. It goes without saying that these are hillside vines near the sea.

This Tuscan location is particularly well suited for the cultivation of international grape varieties, the basis for the blends with which the two main I Greppi red wines are produced.

I Greppi in Bolgheri is characterized by two lakes, the Greppi Cupi lakes, on their property which bolster biodiversity. The lakes attract all sorts of insect and animal life, thus increasing the vitality of the soils and growing conditions.

The farm's proximity to water creates the ideal conditions for extended ripening: Ventilation from the sea helps to cool the fruit during summer months and keep the grape bunches dry and healthy (free from mildew or rot) while also cooling the vineyards.

We've learned the significance of Bolgheri DOC. The other bookend, Castagneto Carducci, is a cooperative municipality in the Tuscan Province of Livorno about 50 miles southwest of Florence and about 30 miles southeast of Livorno. This municipal area is named after the poet Giosuè Carducci, who was an Italian poet, writer, literary critic, and teacher. Carducci was very influential and was regarded as the official national poet of modern Italy. In 1906 he became the first Italian to receive the Nobel Prize in Literature, thus worthy of the namesake municipality.

Castagneto Carducci is linked to the production of fine Italian wines, which have made the wine cellars of Bolgheri and the surrounding area famous throughout the world.

One unique feature is that to get to Bolgheri, you have to drive on a straight scenic road about three miles long, lined by 2,450 majestic and ancient cypress trees which ends in front of the Bolgheri Castle. This boulevard is referred to as Viale dei Cipressi (Boulevard of Cypresses).

This tree-lined road, built in the 19th century, connects the Oratory of San Guido with the historic center of the village of Bolgheri all via a long straight road, with two rows of dense, cypress trees on both sides creating a truly stunning entry into town.

The road was lined with cypress trees under the advisement of Count Guido Alberto. It became famous thanks to the poem *Davanti San Guido* by the poet Giosuè Carducci, who made his home there. In his verses he wrote:

I cipressi che a Bólgheri alti e schietti
Van da San Guido in duplice filar,
Quasi in corsa giganti giovinetti
Mi balzarono incontro e mi guardar.

In English, this verse translates to:

"The cypresses that in Bólgheri are
tall and straightforward
Go from San Guido in two rows,
Giants are almost in the running
They jumped up to me and looked at me."

Usually, to learn about winemaking at our chosen Tuscan wineries we interview the owners, the actual winemakers, the family and others to understand the character and process of Tuscan winemaking.

In the case of I Greppi, we have opted to talk to the news sources, tellers, and purveyors, and understand how I Greppi is advancing winemaking, processes, technology, and culture with the renowned University of California, Davis in the U.S.

Let's investigate advancing wine with a partnership with UC Davis.

I Greppi is committed to advancing the quality and understanding of wine produced in Bolgheri DOC, following the scientific direction and experience of the I Greppi owners. Collaborating with one of the top universities in viticulture and enology with a very research-driven approach will help I Greppi to achieve this goal.

During the most recent harvest, I Greppi welcomed their first intern to the I Greppi vineyard. The University of California, Davis (UC Davis), Department of Viticulture and Enology has provided an opportunity to work with their students. The Department of Viticulture and Enology at UC Davis is world renowned and has been at the forefront of advancing the science of grape growing and winemaking in the wine regions of California and around the world. Many of its graduates have gone on to be leading authorities in the world of wine, and hopefully this Italian connection will continue this trend.

The internship program will allow graduate students and undergraduates in their final year to work within the I Greppi estate, developing new skills in a different cultural environment, and also expanding their knowledge gained at UC Davis.

The goal is to have a long and very fruitful relationship with UC Davis, including many more interns visiting the vineyard over the years, and opportunities to participate in new and innovative viticulture research.

Let's learn more from the interview with the UC Davis/I Greppi intern. This interview is different and comes with an even more unique perspective.

From the perspective of an intern, observations of what typical activities of the chief winemaker are clearly an outsider's viewpoint. This, also, is from a younger, less experienced person entering the wine business. They viewed typical activity as that of paying attention to the overall success in the winery. The approach is having eyes, ears, nose, and palate on the wines every day to help inform decision making to those in charge of each part of the process. It boils down to the importance of following the development of biological processes while they are active during the harvest season and to keep aging wines stable during the wine evolution.

A successful day as a result of those activities is preserving the quality inherent in the grapes. The I Greppi laboratory is used to closely monitor the wines making sure of this quality. There is definitely a preventative nature to quality vs. reacting to a problem, with stylistic decisions made intentionally in line with the pure fruit flavors. Spoken like a true winemaker.

The association with UC Davis and a Tuscany winemaker is unique and serves to enhance both partners. From one UC Davis intern working in Tuscany, "I was the first intern to receive the I Greppi scholarship through my school, UC Davis. What was supposed to be a four month stay has now become a three year endeavor with a much longer stay in sight. Right now, I have the fantastic opportunity to ask the question "What makes our wine special?" I am approaching this question through improvements in quality as well as through our international research project with UC Davis."

As you explore the winery you get to witness and investigate unique techniques, applications, and methods. The best way to understand all that goes on is asking why at each step of the operation. Every day there is more information available about wine and winemaking than there ever has been before whether at I Greppi, in Tuscany, or worldwide.

One of the biggest challenges that non-native people have is living in rural Italy and speaking or learning the language. Once the conversational language level is reached, more language knowledge is picked up and the quality of life increases in association with that.

Culture at I Greppi is very similar to the other Tuscan wineries visited and learned about. It is very important that all involved, employees, owners and others feel a sense of ownership and pride over the wine made. This is especially true in a young DOC like Bolgheri; one that is only 27 years old and famed for being one of the first places to cultivate international wine varieties. It is the middle ground between the old world and the new world of winemaking, incorporating international ideas and furthering the spirit of Bolgheri.

There is lots of talk about the international angle to Bolgheri wines. Moving into New World

Wines is the result of the owners, a young vineyard and things like the partnership and association with UC Davis.

A new generation of winemakers is bringing this historic area to the forefront of wine appreciation and study.

Wines and the winemakers in the New World of Tuscany personify the entrepreneurial spirit you would expect from descendants of immigrants, old-timers, and Old-World inhabitants that struck out searching for a new and better life in new places. In these regions the winemaking practices vary, and there is much innovation and experimentation. The New World generally places less emphasis on the old ways of making wine and more emphasis on making wine that takes advantage of modern advances.

Sometimes you will hear people use the term New World condescendingly, as a way to undermine a wine, preferring the romanticism of the Old World, which we find silly. The current trend in wine is to prefer Old World to New World, just as vintage styles come back into style, but trends come and go in ebb and flow fashion. We think preferences will again swap. This basis of knowledge will help you understand, share, and enjoy as all that happens in the world of Tuscany wines now and in the future.

A Final Celebratory Note: Bolgheri DOC 25th Anniversary

WHETHER YOU ARE an intern in Italy on your second day or a seasoned Tuscan winemaker, there are certain events that fall into the classification of must attend. One of those is the Bolgheri DOC 25th Anniversary dinner where 750+ members of the Bolgheri wine family dined on the Viale di Cipressi.

This huge and beautifully coordinated dinner was organized by the Bolgheri DOC wine consortium. The Bolgheri DOC Consortium celebrated its first 25 years from birth with a sparkling gala dinner along the world-famous cypress-lined avenue that leads to the Tuscan city. This dinner hosted a thousand guests who sat at a half-mile long row of outdoor tables before eating four courses and drinking from a list of 120 different wines.

According to the Wine Protection Consortium, they dedicated three days of meetings, events, and tastings to this anniversary. An hour before midnight, hundreds of guests raised their glasses in final toasts of celebration—of the closing of summer, of harvest, of recent excellent vintages—and as a way of giving thanks to those who craft the beautiful wines.

ACKNOWLEDGEMENTS

ANOTHER BOOK, ANOTHER round of thanks. It is always with a great sense of gratitude that I finish a book and think back to all who helped me get to that point. It then becomes time to spread some thanks. This is the part that tugs on my heart. My heart swells and there is not enough thanks to go around to my many supporters.

First and foremost, as usual, is my wife Julie. It is she that helps me get to any point in life. She cheers, motivates, and supports any and all things that I do. Fortunately we do it together and that is gratitude at its finest. Behind every good man there is a great woman. She is the great behind my good. I love you, Julie Ann.

Daughter Allison is always by my side whether physically present or at a distance in her travels emulating the philosophy that we share... living the dream. This book is another dream: a labor of love, a fulfillment of my desire to be creative, to contribute and to share. Of course, also in the background but also a part of my life, my thanks to Bradley and Courtney. I love you all.

To assemble a project like this takes a team. A big hats off goes to them. They make me look good as they take this craft to a new level. Thanks to Cathi Stevenson and Gwen Gades for their cover design, formatting, and guidance in this area.

A big thank you goes out to the many Tuscan winemakers that I interviewed. Valeria Zavadnikova, Ilaria Anichini, Conte Sebastiano Capponi, Ivan and Sabrina Malpaga, Leonardo Beconcini, Eva Bellagamba, Daniele Rosti, Francesco Carletti, Maria Stella Carletti, Khanh Nguyen, Franco Batzella, Matteo Gambono, Keaton Crow, and Miriam Caporali were all instrumental with their insight, knowledge, desire to share with me, and their lives as Tuscan winemakers. Thank you and for the next time I see you, I look forward to saying Grazie! in person.

Little did I know that my travels to Italy would enlighten me with their history and fuel my desire to learn more. Our world is a small place and we are here for a short time. Pursuing different passions on an international basis has taken me to Italy and the Tuscany region. I look forward to my next visit there and to learning even more.

All in all, thank you to all who support me on my journeys. Thank you for allowing me to share and to be gratified. I only hope that I can return the same to any and all in the future.

Lastly, Nola and Ivy are always by my side in their own animalistic lives. They know that I thank them. Just count their daily treats.

And then there's Lu.

ABOUT THE AUTHOR

Al Lautenslager is a seven-times published, best-selling author, entrepreneur, book collector, businessperson, and professional speaker who is passionate about Italy, Da Vinci, and Renaissance history. He has traveled to Italy to see Renaissance History and Tuscan life in full view, in the Tuscan winemaker's own country/region. He has lived a life like many Italians, like da Vinci as an engineer and writer, with multi-disciplined interests, curiosities, and skills. His pursuit of art, Italian food and drink, and Da Vinci history comes from the research for this book and the many Italian history and travel books in his collection.

Sources

I: Introduction
The Agony & Ecstasy by Irving Stone 1961.

III: Is Tuscany a State?
https://en.wikipedia.org/wiki/Sangiovese

http://www.banfiwines.com/region/italy/tuscany

IV: Wine Passion
https://archivio.letitwine.com/en/tell-wine-stories-about-passion-for-wine/

https://my.boissetcollection.com/basicproduct/passion-wine-book

V: Why Do People Like Italian Wine?
https://www.newyorker.com/science/maria-konnikova/what-we-really-taste-when-we-drink-wine

VI: TUSCANY PASSION
La Passione: How Italy Seduced the World
by Dianne R. Hales 2019.

The Italians by Luigi Barzini, Atheneum. 1977.

VII: TRADITION
https://en.wikipedia.org/wiki/Tradition

https://www.italianpod101.com/
blog/2021/04/23/italian-culture/

https://www.senato.it/documenti/repository/
istituzione/costituzione_inglese.pdf

VIII:TUSCANY THOUGHTS
La Passione: How Italy Seduced the World
by Dianne R. Hales 2019.

IX: ITALIAN CHIANTI
*Chianti Classico: The Search for Tuscany's Noblest
Wine* by Bill Nesto and Frances Di Savino 2016.

https://en.wikipedia.org/wiki/Francesco_Redi

XI: WINEMAKING AS A CAREER
https://www.wsetglobal.com

XIII: CAMPOCHIARENTI
https://www.campochiarenti.it

https://en.wikipedia.org/wiki/St._Nicholas_
Church_Demre

https://johnfodera.com/category/winemaker-interview/

XIII (A): ITALIAN WINE BUREAUCRACY
https://www.forbes.com/sites/johnmariani/2018/06/07/have-the-italian-wine-regulations-become-a-sham/?sh=44b8e9e527f4

https://islandora.wrlc.org/islandora/object/1213capstones%3A234

XIII (C): ITALIAN FAMILY LIFE
https://www.fluentu.com/blog/italian/italian-sayings/

https://en.wikipedia.org/wiki/Nuclear_family

XIV: CASA SOLA
https://www.casasolawinery.com

https://en.wikipedia.org/wiki/Genoa

https://www.travelandleisure.com/trip-ideas/agriturismi-italys-best-affordable-spots

XV: VALDIPIATTA
https://www.valdipiatta.it/en/

https://grapecollective.com/articles/the-noble-wine-vino-nobile-di-montepulciano-miriam-caporali-and-valdipiatta

https://www.loimer.at/en/

XVI: LA MATTERAIA
http://www.lamatteraia.com

https://www.wine-searcher.com/m/2021/03/
climate-change-threat-to-wine-regions

*Da Vinci Visits Today: A Renaissance Genius
Observes Today's World* - Al Lautenslager 2020.

XVII: MONTEMAGGIO
https://www.montemaggio.com

XVIII: BATZELLA
https://www.batzella.com

XIX: BECONCINI
https://www.pietrobeconcini.com/?lang=en

https://www.jwine.com/about/vineyard-
practices/clones

XX: VILLA CALCINAIA
https://www.conticapponi.it/calcinaia/

XXI: POLIZIANO
https://carlettipoliziano.com/en/

XXII: I GREPPI
https://igreppi.com

https://www.italyandwine.net/blog/bolgheri-
25-years-anniversary

http://www.casoneugolino.com/en/giosue-
carducci-and-castagneto/

Made in the USA
Middletown, DE
13 January 2022